INDIA
Lahore
PAKISTAN
Indus
DELHI
NEPAL
Kanpur
Ganges
Ahmadabad
Calcutta
Narmada
Tapti
Bombay
Godavari
Hyderabad
Arabian Sea
Goa
Panjim
Krishna
Bay of Bengal
Bangalore
Madras
Sri Lanka
COLOMBO
Indian Ocean
N
0
500 km

GOA
Tirakol
Arambol
Pernem
Chapora
Kansarpal
Chapora
Vagator
Anjuna
Mapusa
(Mapuca)
Bicholim
Mayem
Carambolim
Baga
Saligao
Calangute
Sanquelim
Aguada
Mandovi
Panjim
(Panaji)
Old Goa
Gaspar-Diaz-
Beach
Dona Paula
Pilar
Priol
Farmagudi
Bondla Wildlife
Sanctuary
Mormugao
Vasco da Gama
Curtorim
Ponda
Bandora
(Bandode)
Kawale
Molem
Zuari
Borim
Dudhsagar Waterfalls
Cansaulim
Margao (Madgaon)
Colva
Benaulim
Molem
National Park
Sanvordem
Sanguem
Zambaulim
Arabian Sea
Sal
Betul
Fatorpa
Cabo Rama
Fort
Agonda
Canacona
Palolem
Cotigao Wildlife
Sanctuary
N
0
10 km

Practical Travel A to Z

GOA

(India)

1992

Hayit Publishing

<1st> Edition 1992

UK Edition: ISBN 1 874251 25 8
US Edition: ISBN 1 56634 010 1

Author: Hilke Maunder
Translation, Adaption, Revision: Scott Reznik
Print: Druckhaus Rombach, Freiburg/Germany
Photography: Hilke Maunder, Uwe Turek
Distribution to the trade:
UK: Amalgamated Book Service/Kent
USA: National Book Network/Lanham, MD

Printed in Germany

Using this Book

Books in the series *Practical Travel A to Z* offer a wealth of practical information. You will find the most important tips for your travels conveniently arranged in alphabetical order. Cross-references aid in orientation so that even entries which are not covered in depth, for instance ''Holiday Apartments,'' lead you to the appropriate entry, in this case ''Accommodation.'' Thematically altered entries are also cross-referenced. For example, under the heading ''Medication,'' there appear the following references: ''Medical Care,'' ''Travel Medications,'' ''Pharmacies,'' ''Vaccinations.''

With travel guides from the series *Practical Travel A to Z* the information is already available before you depart on your trip. Thus, you are already familiar with necessary travel documents and maps, even customs regulations. Travel within the country is made easier through comprehensive presentation of public transportation and car rentals in addition to the practical tips ranging from medical assistance to newspapers available in the country. The descriptions of cities are arranged alphabetically as well and include the most important facts about the particular city, its history and a summary of significant sights. In addition, these entries include a wealth of practical tips — from shopping, restaurants and accommodation to important local addresses. Background information does not come up short either. You will find interesting information about the people and their culture as well as the regional geography, history and the current political and economic situation.

As a particular service to our readers, *Practical Travel A to Z* includes prices in hard currencies so that they might gain a more accurate impression of prices even in countries with high rates of inflation. Most prices quoted in this book have been converted to US$ and £.

Contents

Registry of Places

Agonda 13
Aguada 14
Anjadiv 15
Anjuna 15
Arambol 16
Arvalem 17
Baga 18
Baina 19
Bandora (Bandode) 20
Benaulim 22
Betul 23
Bicholim 23
Bondla Wildlife Sanctuary 24
Borim 24
Cabo Rama Fort 24
Calangute 25
Canacona 27
Cansaulim 28
Carambolim 28
Chandor 28
Chapora 30
Chorao Bird Sanctuary 30
Colva 34
Cotigao Wildlife Sanctuary 36
Curtorim 40
Dabolim 40
Dona Paula 41
Dudhsagar Waterfalls 43
Farmagudi 45
Fatorpa 45
Gaspar Diaz Beach 47
Goa Velha 48
Kansarpal 60
Kawale 61
Mapusa (Mapuca) 62
Margao (Madgaon) 63
Mayem 65
Molem National Park 67
Mormugao 68
Old Goa 70
Palolem 80
Panjim (Panaji) 80
Paroda 90
Partagal 92
Pernem 93
Pilar 94
Ponda 96
Poverim 96
Priol 98
Saligao 102
Sanguem 103
Sanquelim 103
Sanvordem 104
Sirigal (Sirigao) 105
Talaulim 107
Talpona 108
Tambdi Surla 108
Tirakol 112
Vagator 119
Valpoi 119
Vasco da Gama 119
Zambaulim 124

General Information

Accommodation 10
Agrashala 13
Bakshisch 20
Banks 21
Beaches 22
Cinema 32
Climate 33
Clothing and Equipment 34
Crime 36
Cuisine 36

Currency 39
Customs Regulations 40
Drinking Water 41
Driving and Traffic 42
Drugs 42
Economy 43
Electricity 44
Embassies 44
Geography 47
Guided Tours 49
Gurudwara 50
History 50
The Beginning of a Legend .. 50
Canons, Churches
and Commerce 52
Parting with Paradise? 56
Holidays and Celebrations 57
Information 60
Insurance in case of illness 60
Language 61
Maps 62
Markets 65
Medical Care 66
Museums 68
Music 69
National Parks 69
Nudity 70
People 92
Photography 93
Postal System 96
Press 97
Prohibition 100
Religion 100
Shopping 104
Spices 105
Sports 106
State and Government 107
Telephone 108
Temples 109
Time of Day 110
Tourist Information 112
Transportation 113
Travel Documents 117
Travel Literature 118
Travelling to Goa 118
Vegetation 120
Wildlife 122

Accommodation

The atmosphere of apprehension, resulting from the colonial times can still be perceived: in all of India no purely foreign firms are allowed. At least two thirds of a company's capital must be in Indian hands. These principles of majority proportions within joint ventures can be applied to managers or the simplest of maids. An example: the American hotel multi-national Sheraton is behind the largest Indian hotel chain Welcome Group. The second condition in the licence contract is that the profit must be invested in India. This is to prevent the hard currency earned from the tourist industry from flowing out of the country, without the host country being able to profit from the tolerated boom in tourism. At first glance, it seems that this policy is quite noteworthy for a third world country. However, if one analyses the situation more closely, then a vicious circle becomes apparent: the more Goa becomes popular with tourists, the more hotel complexes are crowded along the beaches. The economic blessing becomes a curse.

The consequences can be seen everywhere in Goa *(→History / Parting from Paradise).* Within three years since the expansion of the western package-tour industry Goa's accommodation capacity has grown to over 270 tourist complexes with over 11,000 beds. The trend remains steady and on the rise. However, only 14 of these complexes, including family accommodation, meet the high standards set by western sun worshippers. Only five of them can really be considered luxury holiday domiciles, clearly set off by a stylish ambience, exquisite cuisine and unassuming, courteous service — and of course by their price: ten percent is added to the price of a room by the government as a luxury tax and, as a rule, the invoice must be paid in hard currency. Those who would like to find their accommodation on their own can refer to the brochure "Accommodation in Goa" published by the Directorate of Tourism, Panjim. This brochure includes information on the name, location and price of the accommodation. The entries are subdivided into four categories according to standard. Because the number of hotels available rapidly changes from season to season, the following includes only hotels which are offered by the western tourist industry. Additional accommodation can be found under the individual city entries as well as under the heading "Agrashalas."

Unchallenged for years in its top position is a hotel which is not only the highest in price (1000 Rs per night), but also has the greatest dimensions that Goa's

Picturesque: a small pond reflects the palm trees in Salcete, Goa's southernmost province ▶

hotel industry has to offer: the rambling complex of the **Fort Aguada Beach Resort** towers 200 metres over the Sinquerim Beach, the southern portion of the Calangute Beach. Together with the villa complex **Aguada Hermitage,** it counts worldwide as India's best beach resort. With an additional 32 cottages, the **Taj Holiday Village,** a gigantic complex for over 600 guests, employs almost as many service personnel as there are guests. Caring for the gardens alone are 50 gardeners. Built on the ruins of the Fort Aguada, this gem of the Alcon Group offers, in addition to optimal standards, not only excellent sports and recreation facilities, but also incomparable culinary works of art. Those who enjoy a holiday full of culinary encounters can blindly trust the menu at the "Seashell Restaurant." Whether it is the "Sarpatel" spicy pork liver, "Vindaloo" marinated in wine vinegar, the fresh tiger prawns in hearty garlic butter, the colourful rice pilafs, the "curries," the "Thalis" or the "Dhosas," all are a treat to the palate. The chefs at Fort Aguada offer the gourmet an never-ending culinary tour, demonstrating the multiplicity of cuisine found on the Indian subcontinent. Those who swear by burgers or fish and chips can also find restaurants to suit their taste. The "Old Anchor Bar" offers lighter meals and exquisite cocktails.

The five other hotels in the luxury category according to international standards are affordable even for the normal tourist (500 to 800 Rs. per night). The red brick **Majorda Beach Resort** (240 beds, Eastern International Hotels Group) on Majorda Beach is a spacious complex with an extensive garden, offering excellent sports facilities. Shuttle buses take hotel guests to nearby Margao. The **Oberoi Bogmalo Beach Hotel** (252 beds, Tradewings Group), located directly next to Bogmalo village with its countless custom tailors (who could sooner be called "express tailors"), combines the internationality of a convention hotel with the amenities of a holiday resort. All rooms have a view of the ocean, but the bathing lagoon off of Bogmalo Beach is rather small and narrow. Only eight kilometres from Panjim is the **Cidade de Goa** complex (202 beds, Welcome Group). It was built according to the plans of the prize-winning architect Charles Correa from 1982 to 1985. It is, however, not advisable to swim off the Cidade Beach, a portion of the Vainguinim Beach across from Mormugao Harbour. The water is often polluted from the oil that is flushed from the docked ships.

In the 1990 season, two more exclusive complexes have opened their doors: The Leela Beach (500 beds, Kempinski Group) is located on the southern portion of Colva Beach near the small village of Mobar. The five-star hotel not only offers outstanding sports and recreational facilities, but excellent restaurants as well: ''La Gondola" serves Italian cuisine, ''The Riverside Wharf," seafood specialities.

Dona Sylvia, the beach resort on the southern part of the Cavelassim Beach, was designed by the renowned architect Charles Correa. The 170 rooms are spread among several white villas with cozy interiors, decorated in post-modern style. The three restaurants in the Ashok Hotel offer Goan, vegetarian and Chinese cuisine.

Included in the first-class hotel category in Goa are **Hotel Mandovi,** formerly the City Hotel in Panjim, **Hotel Fidalgo** also in Panjim and the **Ronil** (116 beds) near Baga Beach. Several two-storied houses with a circular layout and eight rooms each are grouped around a courtyard and swimming pool.

Good middle-class hotels are **Nova Goa** in Panjim, **Hotel La Paz** in Vasco and **Hotel Zuari** as well as the **Penthouse Beach Resort** in Colva, which was completed in 1987 and is especially well-suited for families with children. **The Goan Heritage** (130 beds) was opened in 1987, the first year of the tourist boom in Goa. It is a simple, cozy complex located directly on Calangute Beach.

Still almost a insider tip are the inexpensive bungalows at the **Vagator Beach Resort** below the Chapora Fort in the north. The simple houses are the ideal lodging for families with children, who are officiallly welcome in the larger hotels, but in truth are only tolerated.

Agonda

Agonda is a village in the southern province of Canacona. The kilometre-long sand beach is still off the beaten tourist track. There are, therefore, not yet any beach pubs or lodging in bamboo huts.

Agrashala

Almost every temple is surrounded by ''agrashalas", which are simple quarters for pilgrims. In some places, they are also called ''dharmashalas." These pilgrim quarters offer simple, clean plank beds in larger rooms or dormitories. Although formerly only a small donation was expected from the Brahmans, they now usually have set prices, ranging from five to ten Rupees per night. Another difference from the past is that those who are of other faiths can also stay in the agrashalas as long as they respect and adapt to temple life.

In Goa, five agrashalas offer inexpensive lodging:

* Shri Ramnath Devi Agrashala, Ramnathi, Bandidava, Ponda, Tel: 33
* Shri Shantadurga Devasthan Agrashala, Kavlem, Ponda, Tel: 57
* Manguirish Saunsthan Agrashala, Mangueshi, Ponda, Tel: 31
* Shri Mahalsha Sansthan/Shri Mahalsa Temple Agrashala, Mardol, Ponda
* Shri Nageshi/Shri Nageshi Devasthan Agrashala, Bandora, Ponda

Aguada

Eighteen kilometres east of Panjim, the peninsula of Aguada juts out into the Arabian Sea near the Mandovi River delta. A small spring, which earlier provided the only source of freshwater in the region, was the source of the name Aguada: "agoa" means water.

Aguada / **Sights**

Fort Aguada: Located strategically on the 87 metre-high summit of the "Aguada Point," a peninsula composed of red laterite soil, is the massive Fort Aguada, built by the Portuguese from 1604 — 1612 under the administration of Viceroy Dom Lorenço de Tavora. From this vantage point, it was possible to patrol the Mandovi delta and shipping traffic to the capital. The Portuguese fortified the northern flank of this fort along Sinquerim Beach with an impressive rampart. Of the two bulwarks Maman and D. Maria, only the latter has remained intact. The Portuguese were able to give their enemies a "reception" from the barrels of no less than 79 cannons. On January 2, 1802, the English occupied the fort under the pretext that they were protecting the small Portuguese colony from the French troops. Two years later, in November 1804, they occupied the fort once again staying almost nine years this time. During this period, a hospital and a number of storage rooms were built. These are, however, no longer in existence. After extensive renovations, the damp dungeons of this fort now serve as a civil prison.

The traditional raising of the Indian flag takes place here every year on July 18 to commemorate the "liberation" of Goa from the colonial rulers, an event which was initiated here (as was the conquest itself).

Lighthouse: 13 metres above Aguada is the oldest lighthouse in Asia. Every seven seconds a beam of light races around its circuit. This light beam can be seen by ships at a distance up to 40 kilometres and was once the trademark of the Mandovi. Open from 4 to 5:30 pm.

Aguada Beach: Also called Candolim Beach, this is the southernmost portion of the Calangute Beach.

Air Travel →*Travelling to Goa*

Anjadiv

The 1.6 kilometre long and only 300 metre wide rock island is located in the southernmost costal region of Goa near the border to the Karnataka province. The west coast, mostly steep and rugged, is completely unfertile. On the eastern coast in contrast, there are picturesque villages with coconut, orange and mango plantations. A small spring framed in granite supplies the island with freshwater. As was the case with Fort Aguada, the history of Goa boasts that Goa's liberation in 1961 originated from this island in the Arabian Sea. Up until that time the island served as a Portuguese penal colony for undesirable Goans, who were brought to the island and occupied with knitting socks, thus hindering an uprising against the occupying forces.
The **Fortress** which dominates the island, was erected in 1682 by the Portuguese. In the same year, The Mahrattas under the leadership of Sambhaji tried in vain to storm the fortress and conquer the island from which they had been driven a few years earlier.
The island's **Nossa Senhora des Brotas** church is one of a kind: it has neither priest nor congregation.
Travelling to Anjadiv: The only harbour on the island is located in a small bay in the middle portion of the island's eastern coast.

Anjuna

Almost ten kilometres from Mapusa, Anjuna is home to an event known throughout the world in certain circles: every Wednesday, the hippie market takes place if the police don't decide to stage a raid at that particular time. Merchants come from all over India to sell Indian crafts, souvenirs, knick-knacks and art: women from Rajasthan and Karnataka, their hair, hands, ears and legs covered with heavy silver jewellry and with ivory and plastic bracelets on their arms carry bright red bags, colourful patchwork quilts and camel-hair blankets. Even merchants from Tibet are drawn to this region in winter. They sell silver, jade and hand-made figures of gods carved from talc, wood or other materials. Amid the hubbub, European faces can also be seen: young women in bright homespun clothing; a Swiss lady displays her second-hand corsets on a cord suspended between two palm trees. A crowd forms around George, a man from Southern England, who came to Goa six years ago, married a Goan and now makes his living as a baker. His brownies and doughnuts are truly a treat. Nearby, a blonde Hun shouts in excitement ''real German *Schwarzbrot;*" which is as rare in Goa as François' handmade cheeses.

The traditional Christmas party on the beach attracts globetrotters from all over the world and is as widely known as the weekly flea market.

The narrow sand beach measuring almost five kilometres in length is bordered by **Chapora Fort** in the north. This fort was built by Count Ericeira in 1717 to guard the Chapora River delta. Today, this ruin is a popular observatory for tourists. Two narrow paths lead around the southern coastal cliffs to **Baga:** one, over the mound, the other, along the coast above the sea.

Anjuna / **Practical Information**

Restaurants and Bars: Along the coast, one will find numerous beach pubs and small restaurants. The restaurant's appeal usually depends on the clientele and not on the food. The one restaurant which is popular across the board is the Garden Restaurant which serves excellent fish. Located somewhat secluded and therefore harder to find is ''Gregory's", called ''the star of Anjuna" by the regulars. ''Gregory's" is only open during the evening, but remains open longer and offers western dishes at only slightly higher prices.

Accommodation: In the high season from November to March, the huts are all rented out to those staying for a longer time and the few hotels at the Chapora intersection are completely booked. In short: one must have a bit of luck in finding a room here as well as being willing to wait a day and sleep outside if necessary. For a few Rupees, the restaurant owners will be happy to look after luggage in the meantime. Also to look after certain other arrangements, which attract the more hippie-oriented tourists and police alike ''ganja:" hallucinogenics similar to magic mushrooms, Afghan, hashish biscuits and other substances which tempt into the beyond.

Arambol

Located on the northern border to the Maharashtra province, Arambol is a beach that has not yet made the acquaintance of package tourism. Only a few of those who have bid the conventions of western society a fond adieu have built their huts out of palm mats or have rented out a room from the inhabitants at a ridiculously low price. The beach is divided into two sections. In the direct vicinity of the village with the same name is the broad portion which extends to the mouth of the Chapora River. For ten Rupees, beachcombers can cross the river in fishing boats and continue their expedition through Vagator and Anjuna to Calangute. To the north, the coast becomes more rugged and rocky; small bays predominate. A small pathway leads along the coastal cliffs to the portion of the beach called **Arambol Lake Side,** which was so named because of the freshwater lake which the hippies transformed into a natural washing facility, consequently leading to the lake's pollution. The young westerners are alone among themselves, undisturbed by the curious Indians who journey by the busload to the Vagator, Baga, and Calangute beaches to see the topless white women, snapping pictures with their cheap pocket cameras. Upon returning, these snapshots are sold at horrendous prices.

Arambol / **Practical Information**

Travelling to Arambol: From Mapusa, there is hourly bus service to Siolem. From there, the ferry departs for Chopdem where a bus to Arambol will be waiting.
Food and Drink: Directly in the city, there are around ten Çay-Shops offering simple Indian dishes with strong western characteristics. Halfway to Arambol Lake Side, perched on the cliffs is a popular beach restaurant where the food is quite good.

Arambol Lake Side →*Arambol*

Arvalem

Arvalem is 44 kilometres north of Panjim in a pastoral landscape of gently rolling hills. According to the legend, the Pandavas once lived here in exile.
Sights
Arvalem Caves: Inscriptions written in Brahmi were found in these caves, proving the existence of the earlier Sanchipure civilisation dating back to around 100 B.C., which was formerly only presumed to have existed. During the excavation work, archaeologists also came across a statue of Buddha. The three main interconnected caves along with the living chambers can be toured.
Arvalem Waterfalls: From the temple caves, a small stairway leads up to a platform, offering the best view of the waterfalls. At this point, the Saleli River

drops 24 metres to the basin below. This is a popular bathing spot with the Indians who take appropriate advantage of the masses of cascading water. The best time of year for a trip to the waterfalls is shortly after the rainy season.

Baga

The northern portion of Calangute Beach is dominated by individualists and those with alternative lifestyles. Even those who hob-nob with the more chic circles enjoy dropping out of society for one or two months during the winter — although usually living in more style than the hippies from the 60's, of which only a few still belong to the hard core, zooming through the landscape on their Harley Davidsons.

Baga / **Practical Information**

Accommodation: The majority of holiday travellers rent inexpensive rooms or huts from the local residents.

Hotels: Baia do Sol: modern hotel with an impressive garden, rooms are located in the main building and in separate cottages.

Riverside cottages, away from the beach located near the river, hotel restaurant, bar, all rooms with mini-bar. More modest,less expensive accommodation can be found in the cottages which also belong to the complex. These are across the river and can be reached by crossing a gargantuan concrete bridge.

Villa Goesa: a small, simple bungalow complex, located two minutes from the beach.

Captain Lobo's Beach Resort: This hotel complex opened in 1988 and includes 30 separate, two-story apartment houses. The bar and restaurant are located in the centre's main building.

Night Life: Coco Banana: Here, disco night takes place every Saturday.

Haystack: Every Friday is show night with food, song and dance for an all-inclusive price of 120 Rs. The establishment is owned by Remo, the most famous pop star in Goa, and who has even composed songs for other European artists. He occasionally will also step up to the stage — whereupon the Goans will clamour for a spot in the torch-lit garden. Reservations are recommended.

Restaurants: "Tito's" (also called Richdavy Restaurant) is located between Baga and Calangute amid the small sand dunes. It has a large terrace, with the name of the owner displayed on the roof. The prices are somewhat higher than in other restaurants. Tito's is a popular meeting point for the chic middle

European social circles — one can experience major and minor television stars first hand. The same is also true for ''Good Luck,'' which is further north along the beach toward Baga Cliff.

Casa Portuguesa: higher price category, mediocre cuisine despite the large selection of Goan/Portuguese dishes.

St. Anthony's: Baga's gourmet locale, especially suited for those with a sweet-tooth.

Jack's Bar & Restaurant: located directly by the entrance to the city.

Baina

The municipal beach of Vasco da Gama, named Baina, located on the mouth of the Zuari, is better suited for strolls than swimming. On the opposite bank is the harbour basin of Mormugao.

Relics from Goas's colonial period: St. Catherine's Chapel, the Church of St. Francis of Assisi and Sé Chathedral (from left to right)

Bakshish

Tips are called "bakshish" in Goa and are always expected and sometimes even demanded quite audaciously. In India, tips are considered the requisite for a service: one does not pay upon completion of the service, as is the case in most other western countries, but rather in advance, as a motivational factor. This is why the service personnel can become grumpy if there is no bakshish after fulfilling a task. Tips should remain in relation to the income structure of the country, even when it might appear to be very little when converted into western currencies.

A rule of thumb: A construction worker earns ten to twenty Rupees per day. Three Rupees for the porter or room service is by no means too little. Temple priests, self declared guides, snake charmers, water carriers and other colourful native characters often demand exaggerated and exorbitant prices, which one should by no means pay — first, pay half the sum demanded.

Bandora (Bandode)

Four kilometres east of Ponda is Goa's oldest Hindu village. In this town, with a population of 7,000, there are a number of significant religious sites worth visiting.

Bandora / **Sights**

Shri Naguesh-Temple: This temple is dedicated to the god Shiva. It houses fantastic wooden carvings depicting scenes and figures from the Ramayana on the one side of the temple's gallery. To the other side, there are scenes carved in the wood which depict the demigods Astadikpal and Gandharva. The following two temples were deliberately built opposite each other.

Shri Mahalakshmi-Temple: This is the realm of the goddess of the Shakti cult. The sect traces its roots back to the Bhagavad-Gita, the core of the national Indian epic Mahabharata. In this work, it is written that a god is not to be experienced through the senses, but only through "bhakti," or trusting devotion. The cult figure of Vishnu's spouse was made of black marble. The Bhagvata sect's Sabhamandap with its Gallery housing 18 of a total of 24 incarnations is a rare example of carved depictions of the god Vishnu in wood. The original can be found today in a museum, having been replaced by a copy. This Mahalakshmi temple is very similar to the main Mahalakshmi temple in Kolhapur. Mahalakshmi is depicted here as a peaceful or "satvika" incarnation of the deity, with a lingam (a phallus, the symbol of Shiva, the god of creative power) depicted on her forehead. In each of her four hands, she carries the symbols of her attributes — a bowl, a shield, a club and fruit. The goddess Mahalakshmi was especially revered by the Shilahara rulers (750 B.C. — 1030 A.D.) as well as the early Kadamba kings.

Ramnath Temple: Ramnath is another name for Rama, the eighth incarnation of Vishnu. Located outside the temple walls is the temple pond. A radiant white Dipmal, a stone lamppost typical of Goa, towers beside the entrance. Both simple and modern lodgings for pilgrims extend to the right and left of the long congregation hall. These are the so-called "agrashalas." There is a stage in the middle of the "sabhamandapa" (the congregation hall), where religious plays are performed on Hindu holidays and during celebrations. The most sacred site in the temple is the "garbhargriha," which houses a peculiarity: next to the pictures of Lakhsmi and of Ramnath is the erect symbol of Shiva, the Lingam.

Shri Kashi Math: Located on a hill is the Hindu monastic school. It is run by the Madhwa sect, which is especially widely represented in the western states of the union.

Bandora / **Surroundings**

Gopal Ganapati Temple: Located on a nearby knoll is the temple dedicated to Ganesha. This temple is called "Farmagudi" by the inhabitants.

→*Farmagudi*

Banks

In Goa, there are almost 300 banks; even in smaller villages, branches of the larger banks are present. The hours of operation are not uniform and are usually dependent on the normal business hours locally. Larger banks offering currency exchange and bank transactions with Europe are:

Bank of Baroda, across from Azad Maidan, Panjim, Tel: 29 91, 30 03. Branches in: Margao, Mapusa, Vasco da Gama, Calangute.

Bank of India, across from Azad Maidan, Panjim, Tel: 29 12; Affiliate in Campal: Tel: 32 68. Branches in Margao, Mapusa, Vasco da Gama.

Central Bank of India, Rua Alfonso de Albuquerque, Panjim, Tel: 23 89. Branches in: Mapusa, Margao, Vasco da Gama.

State Bank of India, Panjim, Tel: 23 04, 24 68. Branches in: Mapusa, Margao, Vasco da Gama, Calangute.

Beaches

Goa's economic capital is its beaches: craggy coasts, along the lonely, still partially undiscovered bays, alternating with sublime sand beaches where one can lose oneself in the sheer dimensions. Then, there are also the lively sections of the coastline, with their benign mayhem, where Indians parade along the coast, play music and watch the sun sink behind the waves of the Arabian Sea, transforming the beach into an Indian Corso. The rocky coast gives way to impassable beaches constantly churned up by the sea, where fishermen have built their storage huts made from coconut mats. Every evening they vie with the powerful surf, pushing their heavy, dark boats out to sea, returning the next day, their boats laden with squid, pomfret, kingfish and other delicacies from the sea.

The tourists are still concentrated on the portions of the beaches surrounding the hotels, where enterprising inhabitants have already recognised a new money-making venture. "Ear cleaning, Ma'am?" They call out at a distance, with a small, cotton-shrouded metal stick poised, then immediately commence with their version of aural hygiene. An exclamatory "You very dirty!" ensues, with a tone of repulsion, and with an elegant gesture of the hand, the resourceful Goan conjures a pebble out of the ear and into his palm. "One Rupee extra, Ma'am..." Skillfully balancing their wares on their heads, young girls perpetually sing the praises of chilled soft drinks, cola, fruits — sometimes watermelons, sometimes bananas or mangoes. Even at a distance, a rolled-up towel betrays the would-be masseur; the bright clothing, the merchant from the neighbouring town of Karnataka. They sell saris, lunghis (thin, cotton scarves, infinitely versatile and therefore found in the luggage of any true Goa fan) and bags decorated with pieces of mirror. Here in Goa it is possible to stroll for hours along the fringe of the waves, warm water of the Arabian Sea washing over one's feet, without encountering another soul. Every beach has its own unmistakable character.

→*Agonda, Anjuna, Arambol, Baga, Baina, Calangute, Chapora, Colva, Dona Paula, Gaspar-Diaz, Palolem, Vagator*

Benaulim

Benaulim is a quiet sand beach interrupted by small villages, located two kilometres south of Colva near Colva Beach.

Benaulim / **Practical Information**

Accommodation: L'Amour Beach Resort: Rooms with bathrooms and electric fans, adjacent restaurant, located near the beach.
O Palmar Beach Cottages: across from the L'Amour Beach Resort, near the beach, rooms with bath and electric fans. If there is no one at the reception, check at ''Pedro's" beach restaurant.
Brito's Tourist Home: in the centre of town, 10 minutes to the beach, large complex with simple, clean rooms.
Palm Grove: next to Dominik's Bar.
Trinity High School: often completely booked because of the small number of very inexpensive rooms, 20 minutes to the beach.
Restaurants: Recommendable smaller snack bars and fast-food restaurants are Bar Dominik, Sailor's Bar, Seshaa Restaurant, Satkar Tea House, Mayrose Restaurant and Fridola's Restaurant. In addition, Benaulim offers numerous restaurants, varying greatly in quality. Those which can be recommended are the popular beach restaurant ''Pedro's," despite the extremely slow service, as well as the hotel restaurant in the L'Amour Beach Resort, offering excellent food, albeit in small portions.

Betul

Betul is a picturesque fishing village at the end of Benaulim Beach. The harbour, at the mouth of the Sal River is only used for sailing and fishing vessels due to the water's inadequate depth (less than 10 metres).

Beverages →*Cuisine*
Bhagwan Mahavir Sanctuary →*Molem*

Bicholim

37 kilometres north of Panjim near the Mandovi is the capital city of the province which carries the same name. The town of Bicholim, with its population of around 10,000, is known well beyond the borders of Goa: it is here that magnificent brass lamps, candle holders and bowls are produced.

Bicholim / **Sights**

Namazgah Mosque: This mosque was built by Akbar, the son of Auranzebs as a memorial to the historical battle of 1683 in which Akbar and Sambhaji fought together against the Portuguese.

Surroundings: The recreational area Mayem Lake *(→Mayem)* is located five kilometres away.

Bondla Wildlife Sanctuary

The smallest of the three wildlife parks was founded in 1961. It is called Bondla Wildlife Sanctuary and encompasses 35 square kilometres. Appropriately, a quote from Indira Gandhi is displayed on a large sign at the main entrance: "The survival of man is dependent on the survival of plant and animal life." To the north, the Mahadei River and to the east, the Ragado River flow through the wildlife preserve in the foothills of the Westghats. In the small wildlife shelter "Bondla Zoo," in addition to the porcupine and tiger, a common European pigeon is also displayed behind bars. A small botanical garden is still under construction, but the rose beds and greenhouse have already been completed. Within the extensive wildlife park, a natural slope of the Westghats with hiking paths and picnic areas makes the perfect setting for observing the wild animals.

Borim

Borim is a village comprised of seven hamlets along the street connecting Ponda and Margao. It is located about 12 kilometres from Margao.

Surroundings

Siddhanath Hill: From the west, a serpentine footpath leads through banana, cashew and coconut groves up to Butal Peak (elevation: 410 metres). The exerting climb is rewarded with an impressive panorama: the view extends from the prominent harbour of Mormugao in the north to Fort Caba da Rama in the south.

Buses *→Transportation*

Cabo Rama Fort

The southernmost Fort protecting the coast, the Cabo Rama Fort was built by King Sudem. In 1763 it was seized by the Portuguese. 21 canons served as defence. In the innermost portion of the fort, two springs bubble up from the ground, each with a different water temperature.

Calangute

''The Queen of Goa" extends nine kilometres and is the most famous beach of Goa. It begins in the south directly behind Fort Aguada, which once patrolled the entrance to Old Goa from the Mandovi River and also inspired the name of the luxury beach hotel **Fort Aguada Beach Resort.** The individual portions of the beach each have a different name. **Sinquerim Beach** and **Fort Aguada Beach** are followed by **Candolim Beach,** until one reaches the small town of **Calangute** located approximately in the middle portion of the beach after which the town was named. Seven hamlets belong to this 1107-hectare township, in which 9600 residents were registered during the 1981 census. There is a high level of activity in this town around the clock. Restaurants, pubs, inexpensive tourist accommodation, souvenir shops, travel agencies and even a small library have all settled into this town. Next to the bus station is the small parish church **St. Alexis** stifled by shacks, buses and bars. This church was commissioned by Jeromo do Espirito Santo in 1595. Despite extensive additions around 1710, the original church was demolished and replaced by the present construction. Nothing remains of the four Hindu temples Santeri Sitalnatha, Saptanatha, Brahmanatha and Vetal, which were destroyed by the Portuguese.

Important Note: Petty crime is especially common in Calangute due to the Indian and foreign drug addicts. Money and passports can be deposited at the Bank of Baroda.

Calangute / **Practical Information**

Accommodation: Finding a room is no problem in Calangute. Lodgings suiting every taste and budget can be easily found. If staying for a longer period of time, it is worthwhile to rent a small palm hut or for larger groups, a colonial villa. One inexpensive alternative are the state-run tourist cottages on the main street leading to the beach; simple and relatively clean. Tel: 2 41.

Another inexpensive alternative are the guest houses belonging to Angela P. Fernandes and P.V. Fernandes located directly on the beach. The Sea View Cottages on the way to Baga are available with or without bath.

Library: On the left-hand side of the dead-end road midway between town of Calangute and Calangute Beach is a small library. For a modest fee and with few formalities one can check out books that were donated, merely forgotten by tourists or come from the owner's private collection.

Night Life: A party can always be found in one of the beach huts, a pub or a private villa. If one is not quite courageous enough to simply barge in on

KONKANI SHOULD BE
MADE
OFFICIAL

a party, a stroll along the beach will be sufficient to gain access to the festivities. For years, the undisputed highlight among the insiders is the Saturday Party at ''Coco Banana."

Pharmacy: Calangute Pharmacy, Beach Road.

Restaurants: Restaurant Souza Lobo: excellent food, speciality: ''tiger claws" for 3.50 Rs.

Tourist Hotel: East Indian cuisine at moderate prices, large terrace with a view of the beach.

Alex Cold Drink House: right behind the Tourist Hotel, popular breakfast locale because of its ''lassi" cocktails.

Sea View Restaurant: near the Tourist Hotel, good food served in small portions.

Coconut Inn: better known as ''Dieter's."

Transportation: Between the town of Calangute and the beach one kilometre away, a shuttle service operates regularly from early mornings to late evenings. The central bus station for regional transportation to Mapusa and Panjim is located across from the St. Alexis parish church.

Travel Agency: Spaceway Travels, MGM Space Travels

Camping →*Accommodation*

Canacona

The small town of Canacona in the southernmost province of Goa was still a rare insider tip only two years ago. It has since steadily developed into a tourist centre which is still largely dominated by the more or less hippie-oriented crowd. Worth seeing is the **Shri Malikarjuna Temple.** Presumably built in the mid 16th century by descendants of Kashatriya Samaj, this temple was restored in 1778. In addition to the Shivalingam, 60 deities are worshipped in this temple.

Lodging: Canacona Forest Rest House, Poingini.

Canacona Island →*Palolem Beach*

◀ *An Indian woman in front of one of the numerous examples of graffiti demanding that Konkani be declared the official language in Goa*

Cansaulim

Cansaulim is a small village with a train station near Velsao Beach, the northernmost section of the Colva Beach. **Cansaulim Hill,** a small hill with a gravel road leading up to the plain baroque church on its summit, offers a majestic view. To the north, one can see the Mormugao peninsula and, off the coast, the uninhabited St. Jorge Island, Cambrian Island and Small Island. To the south, Colva Beach stretches to the horizon.

Carambolim

The small village or Carambolim in the Satari Province is around seven kilometres from Valpoi and was originally called ''Chandiwade.''

Carambolim / **Sights**

Brahma Temple: A deity less popular among the people is worshipped here: Brahma, the earth spirit. The shrine is presumed to be from the fifth century. The statue of this deity was brought from the town with the same name, Carambolim near Old Goa, to protect it from the Portuguese. The granite statue presents a typical depiction of Brahma: his face looks into all four directions. In addition to feminine forms, ''Hamsa,'' the goose which he rides is also included on the pedestal.

Carambolim Lake: This small lake, a popular destination for short trips or picnics, holds a botanical peculiarity: red and white lotuses blossom here simultaneously.

Car Rentals →*Transportation*

Chandor

Chandor is a small train station in Salcete, Goa's southernmost province. It lies on the railway to Bangalore, about ten kilometres from Margao. Located here is the oldest colonial governmental seat, which has been opened to the public.

Chandor / **Sights**

The Menezes-Bragança Family Manor: The Menezes-Bragança family descended from a line of high officials and governors from the Portuguese colonial period. They built this stately residence between 1700 and 1750. 28 wrought iron balconies ornament the whitewashed facade. It is, however, risky to set foot in this manor house at present: the floors, made from old teakwood planks, are dangerously rotted. Eight of the balconies lead to the "blue salon," the obligatory mirrored hall of the Bragançan country residence. The lead crystal mirrors are spotted with age, but the massive chandelier made from Venetian glass, the velvet tapestries with their intricate patterns and the artistically inlaid parquet floors echo the joviality of former festivities and awaken an impression of the Lusitanian power and influence.

The ballroom's foyer, where, earlier, the lord of the manor received his provincial overseer as well as envoys and clergymen, is a veritable museum of curios of the past century. Nothing has been changed since original construction. Trinkets and gifts, porcelain and books, post cards from the present and letters from the past — everything was given its own place of honour in this room: gathering dust in a drawer or display case, hung on the walls or strewn about on the tables, benches, chairs and trunks. The small sofa for courting couples is very interesting: the husband and wife to be would sit only partially facing one another, separated by the back of the sofa. To one side was the seat for the chaperone.

The sleeping chamber was intentionally decorated only sparingly. A large oak bed with a nylon canopy — the silk canopy is meanwhile reserved for special occasions — dominates the room. A chair, a massive dark wardrobe, a commode with a porcelain basin, a wobbly table and two balconies opening to a view of the small garden and the dusty church square are the only embellishments in this room. A gallery runs along the back wall of the house, partially roofed and partially open. Date palms, yuccas, mallows, small banana shrubs, young coffee bushes and numerous orchids hinder entrance into the jewel of this manor house: the private chapel. Never was a Menezes-Bragança baptised, wed or interred away from the manor. On Sunday and occasionally during the evening, the lord of the manor would hold the services; only on special occasions was the priest from the nearby church asked to lead the services. Colourful Azuelejos and hand-painted tiles ornament the floors. Genuine gold leaf was not only used in decorating the altar with its naive, traditional image of a saint, but the low walls and small door to the chapel as well. The necessities for a religious service are concealed behind the altar, covered with the dust of years gone by. Concealed even farther back is the sacramental wine ...

The Miranda Family's country residence can also be visited if arrangements are made in advance.
→*Sanvordem*

Chapora

Vagator Beach and the small village, located at the mouth of the Chapora, opening to the Arabian Sea are still among the untouched areas in northern Goa. The widely scattered community of Chapora, about 12 kilometres from Mapusa, is hidden in under the thick foliage of the coconut groves.

Chapora / **Sights**

Chapora Fort: The trademark of the town is impressively perched on a hill. The view from this well-preserved Portuguese fortress (built in 1717) is striking: to the north, the lonely bay, to the east the serpentine Chapora riverbed and the slopes of the distant Westghats; to the south Anjuna, and to the west the infinite expanse of the Arabian Sea, dotted with oil tankers heading for Arabia.

Chapora / **Practical Information**

Accommodation: Similar to Anjuna, the lodgings in Chapora are mainly equipped for holiday travellers who stay for longer periods. Therefore, finding a room can become a problem. Because commercial tourism is hardly existent in Chapora, one must be willing to make compromises and lower one's expectations.
Restaurants: Julie Jolly's: popular beach pub serving a small but tasty selection of food.
Lobo's: excellent seafood entrees, limited space, closed Sundays.

Chorao Bird Sanctuary

Established in 1987, Chorao Bird Sanctuary is located about four kilometres up the river from Panjim on Chorao Island in the Mandovi River. A ferry departs hourly for Chorao Island from Ribandor.

Tito's Restaurant on Baga Beach offers, in addition to excellent food, an appealing ambience ▶

Tito's

The natural reserve encompasses 180 hectares of swampland and mangrove forests. 200 species of birds including numerous migratory birds can be found here, as can the meanwhile rare river crocodile, which can grow up to 7 metres in length. Those who would rather explore the water region with the fishermen in their canoes must first be granted official permission from Khazan Singh, Deputy Conservator of Forests, Junta House, Panjim.

Cinema

Not Hollywood, but rather the Indian film industry produces the most films in the world. Approximately 500 to 600 motion pictures are filmed in India every year. Over half of these are produced in Bombay. Even if one does not understand the language, one should definitely treat oneself to an evening at the cinema. Because illiteracy is still widely spread on the Indian subcontinent, most of the Indian films offer realistic down-to-earth entertainment. Slapstick and tragic drama, romantic and action films are brought into such an unmistakable mixture that these films were given a special name: ''Masala" films. These films are created in the same way the spice is carefully composed from the most diverse ingredients; they do not place high demands on the intellect: they entertain and provide diversion from everyday routine.

Large, brightly coloured posters providing information on the current cinema programme are displayed everywhere. Because the Indians love their cinema, it is advisable to buy tickets well in advance of the showings. An attempt to reserve tickets by telephone will usually prove unsuccessful. There are four showings daily.

Cinemas in Goa

Panjim: Cine Samrat/Ashok
Cine El Dorado, Tel: 29 27
Cine National, Tel: 25 65
Vasco da Gama: Cine, Tel: 22 57
El Monte, Tel: 24 39
Margao: Cine Lata
Cine Metropole, Tel: 21 68
Cine Vishant, Tel: 25 58
Mapusa: Cine Alankar
El Capitan
Ponda: Aaisha
Calangute: Cine Shantadurga

Ribandar: Gulmarg
Churchorem: Cine Prashant
Niagara Cinema
Cine Shamim
Sanquelim: Cine Sanquelim

Climate

Goa has hot and humid weather during the entire year. From June to the beginning of September, monsoons transform the countryside into one huge desert of mud; diseases and epidemics reach their peak. The seas are so rough that swimming in the ocean would mean certain death. In recent years, however, there were no monsoons. From October to the end of April, the western tourists head for Goa's fabulous beaches. The most beautiful time of year is from November to March. In December, Indian honeymooners invade Goa, resulting in double bookings at the hotels.

Climate Table in °C (°F)

Month	**Minimum**	**Maximum**
January	19.8 (67.7)	32.1 (89.8)
February	20.4 (68.7)	31.8 (89.2)
March	22.8 (73.0)	32.3 (90.1)
April	26.3 (79.3)	33.1 (91.6)
May	24.3 (75.7)	33.3 (91.9)
June	23.9 (75.0)	30.2 (86.4)
July	23.9 (75.0)	28.8 (83.8)
August	23.5 (74.3)	29.2 (84.5)
September	23.5 (74.3)	29.5 (85.1)
October	23.6 (74.5)	31.3 (88.3)
November	21.8 (71.2)	32.8 (91.0)
December	20.2 (68.4)	32.7 (90.9)

Monthly precipitation ranges between 304 and 381 mm (between 12 and 15 inches), usually during the monsoon season from July to September. The average yearly precipitation is around 3500 mm (138 inches).

Clothing and Equipment

It is consistently warm and humid during the entire year in Goa. For this reason, any clothing made from synthetic fabrics should be left at home. It is recommended to pack light and loosely fitting cotton, silk and linen clothing. White articles of clothing are also better left at home since they take on a grey-blue tinge after being washed in Indian detergents. T-Shirts, brightly coloured skirts and leisurely shirts can also be purchased very inexpensively in Goa. The markets, stands and street merchants offer an abundance of inexpensive clothing. One should also definitely pack swimming gear since nude bathing is not only considered uncivil by the public but is also prohibited by law. For evening outings to restaurants or night clubs, men should bring along long trousers and a long-sleeved shirt and necktie. It is considered highly uncouth to go into a nicer restaurant with an open collar. Women wearing shorts risk being asked to leave. Because the air conditioning in most of the restaurants runs at full capacity, it is wise to bring a light jacket, a cardigan or a sweater along.

Light shoes and sandals are the most appropriate shoes for this region. In addition, the Goan shoemakers have an incredible knack in making high-quality copies of western shoes at an incredibly low price — pack your favourite pair and have a similar pair made in Goa. The same is true of the tailors, who have set up shops near the larger hotels.

One should by all means bring along photo equipment and film including a film-safe container.

Furthermore, insect repellent is difficult to find in Goa, as are hygienically packaged tampons or sanitary napkins and hand cream.

An adapter set with different types of plugs is a very useful item to bring because Goa has a chaos of sockets and plugs.

For visiting the temples it is wise to bring a large scarf which can be draped over exposed shoulders.

Colva

In the south, Goa's longest beach stretches over 25 kilometres. It is often compared with the Brazilian Copacabana. Here too, the individual sections of the beach have different names. The northern end, **Velsao Beach,** is quiet and orderly; the commotion begins at **Majorda Beach,** with its generous hotel complex with the same name, built in accordance with the local architectural style. In contrast, a building boom is already raging in the main town of **Colva.** The activity is most vigorous on this portion of the beach. Colva Beach ends at the mouth of the Sal River. During low tide, one can safely wade across to **Betul Beach.**

Every year in October, the Christian population of Goa celebrates the "Fama," a religious folk festival lasting several days, which is in honour of the Christ child. In the procession, a picture of the miraculous baby Jesus is carried under a canopy from the Our Lady of Merces church (located directly on the road to Margao), winding along a complicated route through the town to the beach and then back to the church.

A statue of the local Hindu deity, the goddess Ravalnatha, was brought to safety in Talaulim to protect it from the Portuguese, where a second temple was built in honour of this goddess.

Colva / **Practical Information**

Accommodation: Colva offers a wide selection of lodging. The less expensive guest houses can be found on the northern section of the beach. The most expensive accommodation is Hotel Silver Sands, Tel: 36 45-6, with three suites and 55 lavishly furnished rooms.

The state-run Tourist Cottages (Tel: 22 87, in the centre of the village) are inexpensive, functional and relatively clean. They offer single and double rooms, a separate dining room and kitchen. In the dormitory, a bed can be had for 15 Rupees per night. The complex has only recently been expanded. Additional accommodation with western standards are: White Sands Hotel, Tel: 32 53, 13 double rooms, 13 suites, dormitory, middle price category; Sea View Cottages; Mar e Sol Hotel; Sukhsagar Beach Resort, Tel: 38 88.

Restaurants: The Dolphin: restaurant in the "White Sands Hotel," located on the beach, traditional Goan cuisine, Portuguese cuisine and seafood specialities.

Vincy's Hotel Restaurant: located on the beach, formerly *the* locale in Colva. Since being renovated, its clientele has tripled, despite the bland food.

Peacock Bar & Restaurant: in Hotel Mar e Sol, hot food and cold beer.

Angelo's Corner: beach restaurant.

Lucky Star Restaurant: located directly on the beach, with the contemporary "beach sound" blaring from a gigantic stereo system.

Lactania Restaurant: next to the Hotel Silver Sands, excellent seafood.

Men Mar Inn: often very full due to its central location.

Nosso Lar Bar & Restaurant: old locale with a great deal of Portuguese flair, reservations in advance are recommended.

Umita Corner Bar & Restaurant: beach pub with videos, some in English.

Johnny's: beach pub, occasionally offers "Buffet & Party" at irregular intervals and organises bus trips to the flea market in Anjuna *(→Anjuna).*

Consulates *→Embassies*

Cotigao Wildlife Sanctuary

Goa's southernmost national park is the Cotigao Wildlife Sanctuary in the Canacona province near the border to Karnataka. It can be reached quickly via the N 17 from Panjim to Mangalore. Its 150 square kilometres are home to the large Gaur herds (often compared to bisons) sambars, chitals and dwarf goats. Also represented in large numbers are langurs, apes and a few remaining panthers in contrast to the countless porcupines.
Accommodation: Forest Department Guest House.

Credit Cards *→Currency*

Crime

Violent crimes like rape or murder remain a rarity in Goa; theft, in contrast, is almost considered a peccadillo — the victim was simply stupid and careless enough to let himself be robbed, therefore, it was his own fault. On the streets, theft to finance a drug habit is, unfortunately, becoming increasingly common. Therefore: travel documents and valuables should be left in the hotel — the hotels offer the use of their safe for their guests free of charge. On Calangute Beach, passports and money can also be left at the Bank of Barode for safe keeping. In addition, one should observe a general rule: always carry handbags and cameras in front of you. Money belts are better than neck pouches and some small change should always be carried in trouser pockets. Those who flaunt their wealth will be robbed with certainty; those who present themselves cautiously are rarely victimised.

Cuisine

Masala and Seafood

For centuries, Goan cuisine has enjoyed an excellent reputation worldwide. It was deemed especially chic by the Britons to hire a Goan chef. The reason for this was exceedingly simple: while the southern Indian cuisine was purely

vegetarian and the northern cuisine allowed only for poultry and lamb dishes prepared in a Tandoor oven (wood burning oven), the Portuguese introduced red meat to the menus — particularly pork, which was unparalleled on the Indian subcontinent. The Goan cuisine could even offer the powerful British colonial lords an alternative to the traditional Christmas dinner: turkey was substituted with a festive menu including a crispy suckling pig. The pork inad is definitely worth tasting. The delicious sweet and sour Masala is made from tamarind, cloves and cinnamon in a small amount of vinegar mixed with sugar. Among the numerous types of fish, the ''pomfret,'' similar in flavour to sole, is most popular in Goa — prepared piquant as ''pomfret masala,'' boiled or grilled. Kingfish, somewhat milder, is most commonly served as a filet. Crab, lobster, prawns and other shellfish are inexpensive all over Goa. Even in the smallest of beach huts, the seafood is always fresh and prepared in the most diverse ways. These types of seafood are especially delicious when grilled crispy in garlic butter over an open fire. Rice, chapati or naan (thin and thicker flat cakes made from rice flour) are served with the main dish.
''Bebinka'' is the name of a caloric temptation, for which the Goans will drop everything: several layers of dough are marinated in cocoa, honey and vegetable oil, served warm or hot, with or without a scoop of vanilla ice cream. One should forgo unpeeled fruit for dessert as a health precaution. What can be recommended are the papayas sprinkled with lemon juice. Their juice has a settling effect on the stomach. Other recommendations are the fresh mangoes or the small, very aromatic bananas. Dhosas, paper thin pancakes made from rice flour, filled with vegetable ragout, beans or chutney are eaten by the Goans for breakfast or as a between-meal snack.
Of the beverages, one should by all means try ''Lassi,'' a chilled yogurt drink served either plain, sweet or salted. ''Feni,'' the locally distilled cashew liqueur is drunk pure or mixed with ''Limca,'' a yellow soft drink. Most of the Indian wines are more similar to port wine or sherry. The brands ''Golconda'' and ''Bosco'' are the most similar to European wines. Of the beers, only the ''Kingfisher,'' ''London Pilsner'' and ''Lager 77'' brands, sold only in 0.7 litre bottles, can be recommended. All of the other brands have an unfortunate similarity to dishwater — any similarity to beer is reflected only by the name.

Selected Culinary Directory

Aloo Gobi — vegetarian dish made from cauliflower and potatoes, seasoned with caraway and served in a mild curry sauce.
Brinjal — eggplant, usually steamed

Dal — coarse porridge usually made from lentils or peas.
Gajar Halva — carrot halva, commonly garnished with edible silver foil.
Kofta — dumplings
Malai Kofta — meatballs
Palak Kofta — spinach dumplings
Kulfi — rice with milk and cardamom
Palak — spinach poached in oil, served as a salad or as a vegetarian entree with diced cheese.
Paneer — white Indian cheese with a flavour similar to tofu
Toddy — palm juice used in the production of liquor and sweets
→*Spices*

Currency

The unit of currency in India is the Rupee (abbreviated: Rs.). It is broken down into 100 Paisa. The denominations of currency notes is 1, 2, 5, 10, 50 and 100 Rupees; coin denominations are 5, 10, 20, 50 Paisa and 1 Rupee. The constantly changing exchange rate was £ 3.25 ($5.57) for 100 Rupees at the end of March, 1991. The form of the coins differs depending on the value — a help to the large number of illiterates in India. Money can be exchanged at all of the banks and in the larger hotels. Travellers' cheques have a more favourable exchange rate than cash. Be cautious when exchanging money on the black market. The higher the denomination of the note the better the exchange rate — up to 30% better than at the banks.
Bringing Rupees into or taking Rupees out of the country is prohibited by law. An unlimited amount of other currencies may be taken in and out of the country. Amounts in excess of the equivalent of 1000 US dollars must be declared upon arrival. Excess Rupees may be exchanged upon departure if the original exchange receipt is presented. The currency exchange counters at the airport are, however, often closed. Therefore, if staying for an extended period, one should not exchange all of the money at once, but rather only the necessary amount. Eurocheques are not accepted. Most hotels accept the following credit cards: American Express, Diner's Club, Visa and Eurocard/MasterCard.

◀ *A colourful domestic temple: Tulsi pedastal with Parvati, Shiva and their son with the head of an elephant on the back of a bull*

Curtorim

Curtorim is nine kilometres east of Margao, located in the Salcete province. Worth seeing is the **St. Alex Church.** This, one of the oldest churches in Goa, was built in 1597 on the ruins of the foundation of a Hindu temple. Part of the old temple foundation can be clearly recognised.

Customs Regulations

Entry

Articles for personal use are duty-free. These include (per person):
1 pair of binoculars, 1 portable tape recorder, 1 transistor radio, two cassette tape recorders (no radio/recorders!), 1 portable typewriter, 2 cameras with 25 rolls of film, 1 motion picture camera with 10 spools of film. 200 cigarettes or 50 cigars or 250 g of tobacco as well as 0.95 litres of liquor. Bringing narcotics, live animals and plants as well as gold or silver coins is prohibited.

Departure

Souvenirs with a total value of £ 39 ($66) — including Indian silks and carpets — may be taken out of the country duty-free. Exceptions to this are gold, gold plate and gold ligation, or gold bars. Also subject to export tax are indivisible articles, whose value exceeds the limit, for example articles of clothing or jewellry. The taxes for these items are then calculated based on the full value. Taking the following out of the country is prohibited: antiques, meaning objects over 100 years old, animal pelts (tiger and leopards furs, snake skins), peacock feathers and Indian ivory. In accordance with the Washington Agreement for the protection of endangered species, these items may not be brought into Europe or the US either — the customs officials will rigorously confiscate these items (even when the street merchant might quite adamantly deny this).

Dabolim

Dabolim, Goa's sole airport, is about three kilometres from Vasco da Gama and 30 kilometres from Panjim. It was first open to civil air traffic in 1985.

Dabolim / **Practical Information**

Airlines: Indian Airlines, Tel: 27 88, 32 51; Air India, Tel: 40 81, 51 72.
Tourist Information: Tourist Information Counter, Tel: 26 44.
Transportation: Shuttle buses travelling to Panjim are available for 15 Rs. By taxi, the trip costs between 150 and 160 Rs. Transfer buses, run by tour organisa-

tions, will take no additional passengers — not even for a fee. The hotels' airport service costs between 200 and 500 Rs. depending on the distance from the airport.

Dona Paula

Dona Paula is seven kilometres from Panjim in the Tiswadi province on the northernmost bank of the Zuari delta. The name of the beach, which is more suited for strolls than swimming, can be traced to a "fidalga," a woman belonging to Portuguese nobility. In 1682, Dona Paula Menezes donated her land to the Catholic church. This tract extended from Caranzarlem to the Cabo Palace. An inscription in the Cabo Palace chapel commemorates this philanthropical gift. Dona Paula is especially popular in the evening: at dusk, the view of **Mormugao Harbour** and the **Zuari River Delta** on the bay located opposite the small observatory pavilion is stunning. One drawback of this panorama is that, due to illegally dumped oil in the harbour, the water and the beaches are relatively polluted. Despite this, the Goan Ministry of Tourism is planning to develop a natural marine sanctuary here. Up the river, hidden in the palm trees surrounding a small bay, is the Sheraton Hotel's "Cidade de Goa." Even here one is advised not to swim in the ocean.

A large sculpture, erected directly by the entrance to the observatory platform, brought international fame to Dona Paula a few years ago. Baroness Yrsa von Leistner, a famous German sculptor, chose Dona Paula as the location for her work "The Image of India." The sculpture depicts an allegorical couple: the man looks to the west into the past; the woman represents the future, looking to the east.

Dona Paula / **Practical Information**

Accommodation: Prainha Cottages: located directly by the ocean, hotel restaurant, Tel: 40 04; Dona Paula Beach Resort.

Restaurants: O Pescador: There is a wonderful view from this Polynesian restaurant, which offers excellent dining on the terrace, in the garden, or in the dining room at moderate prices. Next to O Pescador is the White Rock Restaurant.

Drinking Water

As a general rule: Never drink water from the tap. The water in the hotels, which is boiled and put into thermos pots, is safe to drink. Because one has no way of knowing how long the rooms stood empty before one's arrival or when the water was placed in the room, one should dump the water down the drain and ask for a new pot. When buying bottled water, one must make sure that the original seal is still intact. The hotel's tap water can be used without reservation for brushing one's teeth.

Driving and Traffic

In Goa, vehicles drive on the right-hand side of the road. The traffic signs and regulations are the same as in Europe — at least officially. Unofficially, everyone drives with a high level of individuality, meaning quite spirited.
Missing rear-view mirrors on buses are normal; instead, young men ride along on the running-boards signalling the distance the driver may back up by whistling at different pitches. Equally clever as dangerous is the substitution of turn signals: the young men hang from the door handles far into the traffic and signal in unambiguous gestures that the bus has the right of way in turning left or right.
Goa's good infrastructure can be credited to the Portuguese, who built the first secured network of roads to connect their strongholds. Today, three national highways transverse Goa. The N 17 Bombay — Karwar runs along the coast from north to south connecting Goa's most important cities, Mapusa, Panjim and Margao. A byway, the N 17A leads from Cortalim, the junction with the N 17 south of the Zuari bridge, to the harbour of Mormugao. The N 4A runs from Panjim via Old Goa and Ponda to Belgaum, a city in the neighbouring state of Karnataka. In 1980, the entire system of roadways in Goa measured 4,380 kilometres.

Drugs

India ranks among the top three countries in the production of narcotics. Drug use is high, even among the natives. Consequently, there are very strictly enforced laws controlling this problem with severe punishment — if one is caught in possession of drugs, he or she will end up behind bars after a quick trial; the verdict of the Indian courts is also accepted in European countries. The guilty party is then deported and registered as having a previous conviction.

Dudhsagar Waterfalls

The most famous waterfalls in India, the Dudhsagar Waterfalls, can only be reached from **Kolem** (train station). From there, a sand street leads through two valleys to the marked footpath leading to the falls. After twenty minutes on foot through the jungle, one will come upon the waterfalls. A visit during the rainy season is the most impressive; after the long dry season, the trickle that remains is rather disappointing. The water plunges 603 metres over several cascades into the Candepar, an arm of the Mandovi. The cascades were named "Dudhsagar milk-water" because of their cloudy, milky appearance, resulting from the silt churned up by the water.

Economy

Agriculture

The leading economic sector of this small region is (still) agriculture. If the monsoon rains bring sufficient moisture, then Goa's farmers can harvest up to twice a year. The Monsoon crops, called "kharif," are planted at the beginning of June and harvested at the beginning of October. The winter crops, "rabi," on the other hand, are mainly dependent on irrigation. These crops are planted in November and harvested at the beginning of March. Almost 40% of the land in Goa is arable. The main crop is rice, the second most important is cashews. Like the papayas, mangoes, bananas, pineapples and coconuts, these are exported abroad. Livestock is not bred in Goa. On the average, a farmer only keeps two water buffaloes, used as pack animals and in ploughing the fields. Fishing, however, plays a very important role in nutrition as well as the economy of Goa. Giant schools of mackerels and sardines regularly approach the Goan coast. Predominantly, the traditional dug-out canoes with outrigger nets are used in fishing. Only very few fishermen have motorised boats or larger cutters. Although at one time Goa is said to have been covered with extensive teak forests, scarcely a quater of these are still in existence. To prevent soil erosion from spreading, the remaining forests are patrolled by the Forest Department who enforce annual quotas for felling timber and afforestation. The controls are, however, hardly effective in preserving the forests, but do affect the second largest sector of the economy: the iron ore mines are all located in the forests of the Westghats.

Mining

The mining industry is concentrated in the area around Ponda. Surface mining is employed to extract magnesium, bauxite silicates and iron ore —

mostly using a work force comprised of women equipped with simple tools and machines or only their bare hands. The Portuguese had already begun with the mining of the mineral resources.

Industry

The industrialization began relatively late in Goa. While Goa was still under Portuguese rule, tyre factories, soap factories and food industries for processing fish, fruit and rice were built. Today, Goa is home to 31 large industries, including chemical plants, sugar refineries and cotton processing plants. An industrial area meeting western standards is currently being developed at the Ponda Industrial Park.

Tourism

The tourist sector still ranks fourth in economic capacity but is becoming increasingly important as a sustaining factor in the Goan economy. In relentless exploitation, tourism speculators continue to develop Goa into a top holiday destination. The times are opportune. Sri Lanka, the former leading competitor has been put out of the competition by the constant uprisings. Meanwhile, British, German and Russian tourists choose Goa as their holiday destination. 800,000 visitors spend their holidays in Goa, albeit only 10% from foreign countries. The trend is on the rise. Thus, planning and development continue — even in spite of public resistance. Seven large hotel complexes have already been built on the most beautiful beaches in Goa. 19 more are under construction. The blueprints for further projects are already on file with international architects awaiting realisation.

Electricity

Usually, 220 Volts is the most common. The electricity does, however, often fail (hotel rooms are always equipped with candles) and there are larger electrical fluctuations which many electrical appliances cannot withstand. One is, therefore, well-advised to travel without any electrical appliances. For instance, leave the electric razor at home. A hair dryer requires an adapter, which is difficult to come by in Goa. It is best to buy the necessary adapters before departure.

Embassies

United States: Shanti Path, Chanakyapuri, New Delhi 110021, Tel: (11) 600651.
United Kingdom: Shanti Path, Chanakyapuri, New Delhi 110021, Tel: (11) 690371.

Canada: 7/8, Shanti Path, Chanakyapuri, New Delhi 110021, Tel: (11) 608161.
Australia: 1/50-G, Shanti Path, Chanakyapuri, New Delhi 110021, Tel: (11) 601336.
→*Travel Documents, individual embassies*

Farmagudi

Farmagudi is 26 kilometres from Panjim, located near the thoroughfare to Ponda. In October 1683, the sudden appearance of the Mahratta King Sambhaji and his sizable army thwarted the first Portuguese attempt to conquer the fort at Ponda. A memorial commemorates this historical event. Worth seeing is the **Shri Gopal Ganapati Temple.** The stone figure of Gopal Ganapati was discovered by a shepherd, whose flocks were grazing on the nearby hill. A small shrine with a thatched roof was built. The temple which stands on this site today was commissioned by Shri Dayanand Balkrishna Bandodkar, Goa's first Secretary of State. The ceremonial dedication of the statue (made from a metal alloy) depicting the deity was on April 24, 1966. The temple is exemplary of the successful synthesis of classical and modern temple architecture.
Accommodation: Tourist Cottages, state-run, with an outdoor restaurant in the garden.

Fatorpa

Fatorpa is a village with a population of approximately 3,000, located 16 kilometres southwest of the provincial capital of Quepem.
Worth seeing is the **Shri Shantadurga (Kunkalikarin) Temple:** During the Portuguese prosecution of the Hindus, the statue of the goddess Shantadurga was brought to safety in Fatorpa from a village in Salcete. Shantadurga, incarnation of the goddess Durga as a messenger of peace, appears on the earth to destroy the evil forces. Hindus and Christians alike present offerings to this goddess. During the annual temple festival "Shantadurga Prasann" in January, the donations are collected and auctioned off to the highest bidder. The revenues collected are used to ensure the livelihood of the Brahman priests. The festival's highlight takes place at night: during the torchlight procession, the goddess is lead through the town on a wooden cart.

Food and Beverages →*Cuisine*
Foreign Currency Regulations and Currency Exchange →*Currency*

Gaspar Diaz Beach

The Gaspar-Diaz Beach is also called **Miramar Beach.** Located three kilometres toward the sea from Panjim, this beach is dominated by active commotion, especially during the early evening around dusk. Indian women plunge into the ocean wearing their saris, motorcycles proudly hum, American hits or pop songs in Konkani, the local language, blare from transistor radios at a deafening volume. The peddlers in the countless mobile street shops try to outbid their competitors with ever-increasing intensity. An idle attempt, considering they all offer the same: "puri," a deep fried pastry filled with bright yellow wheat noodles and a potent masala mixture made from peas, beans or lentils.

Gaspar Diaz Beach / **Practical Information**

Restaurants: Martin's Beach Corner: delicious fresh fish and seafood; The Sunset Pub — famous for its view of Fort Aguada and the Mandovi delta in the evening, when the fiery sphere of the sun sinks into the Arabian Sea; stylish beach hut atmosphere.

Geography

Covering only an area of 3,704 square kilometres, Goa is the smallest state in the Indian Union. Compared to European proportions, Goa, the 23rd state in the union, is exactly as large as the Swiss canton Waadt, or 1.5 times as large as the Grand Duchy of Luxembourg. To the North, Goa is bordered by the massive state of Maharashtra, which tried in vain in 1961 to annex the coastline. To the east and the south, the 100-kilometre-long ridge of the Westghats mountain range makes up the natural border between Goa and the larger state of Karnataka. The maximum expanse between the Arabian Sea and the Westghats is 65 kilometres. The present-day Goa adopted the administration subdivision of the state from the Portuguese unchanged. The eleven former districts, the "concelhos" became the new "talukas" (from north to south): Pernem, Bardez, Bicholim, Satari, Tiswadi, Mormugao, Ponda, Salcete, Sanguem, Quepem and Canacona with Panjim as the capital.

Goa can be roughly divided into four geographical regions: the slopes of the Westghats to the west, the central laterite plateau in the states interior, the fertile river basins, and the coastline.

◀ *Especially worth seeing: the interior of the Menezes-Bragança family residence, built during the colonial period in Chandor*

The Westghats: While the ridge of these mountains lies at an altitude of around 1000 metres, some of the summits reach a height of 1130 to 1276 metres. The slopes, originally covered with teak forests, are used in forestry. In some places, the choice timber has been replaced by the quick-growing eucalyptus to stop the advance of soil erosion and head off the damage from the mining industry.
The Central Laterite Plateau: The interior of Goa is characterised by a 100-metre-high laterite plateau. The rivers have carved their beds deep into the reddish rock. A thin layer of humus covers the igneous rock, on which prairie grass and shrubs grow. Intensive cultivation is hardly possible, only the cashew plantations place limited demands on the soil. The small amount of arable land is most recently being developed to establish industry in this region.
The River Basins and Coastal Regions: In sharp contrast to the central plateau, lush tropical vegetation can be found in the river basins and along the fertile coastline. Intensive agriculture including rice, vegetable and fruit crops mark the landscape. Palm trees sway in the wind. An extensive irrigation system traces through the countryside.
The Coast: As seen from the ocean, it is understandable why Goa's coast rightly carries the epithet "The Indian Riviera:" Along its 106 kilometres, the coastal landscape alternates between long, straight sand beaches, impressive coastal cliffs, secluded bays and broad river deltas.
Rivers: A dense network of rivers runs through Goa. The six short and broad rivers — Tiracol, Chapora, Mandovi, Zuari, Sal and Talpona — all have their source in the Westghats and flow westward toward the Arabian Sea. Because they are passable during almost the entire year, they play an important role in transportation within Goa. The largest river in Goa is the Mandovi, which flows 77 kilometres through Goa. In the lower part of the river are numerous fertile islands, that are intensively used in agriculture.

Goa Velha

The similarity in the name with the Indian name of Old Goa causes confusion among tourists. But: Goa Velha is *not* Vel(h)a Goa (Old Goa) with its collection of churches in the jungle. This is the name of the second imperial seat of the Kadamba kings, built in the 11th and 12th centuries, and also called Chandrapura.

Guest Houses →*Accommodation*

Guided Tours

The government-operated Tourist Information Offices offer guided tours. These can be booked through:

Travel Division, Goa, Daman & Diu Tourism Development Corporation Ltd., Tourist Hostel, Panjim, Tel: 33 96, 39 03. There are five tours offered regularly; drivers, buses and tour guides can also be chartered upon request.

Tour of North Goa: (9 am to 6 pm), 35 Rs., departs daily from Panjim to Mayem Lake with stops at the Shri Datta and Shri Vithal Temples. From Mapusa, the tour route leads along the northern beaches of Vagator, Anjuna, and Calangute before returning to Panjim via Fort Aguada. Also operating daily is the South Goa Tour departing from Panjim: (9 am to 6 pm), 35 Rs. After a visit to the main churches in Old Goa, the 400-year-old Mangueshi Temple and the nearby Shri Shantadurga Temple, the trip continues to Margao and from there, further on to Colva Beach. On the return trip, stops are made at the Pilar Monastery as well as the beaches at Dona Paula and Miramar. A "Beach Special" is offered as an afternoon outing for 20 Rs. The tour includes stops at the beautiful beaches of Calangute, Anjuna, and Vagator. The famous Dudhsagar Waterfalls are the final destination of the "Dudhsagar Packages" which depart from Panjim at 7 am, 7:15 am and 8 am according to demand. The "Holiday Special" includes day-trips to Bondla Wildlife Sanctuary, to Tiracol Fort combined with a stop at the nearby Arambol Beach and to the jungle temples of Tambdi Surla. Prices for these tours range from 20 to 40 Rupees.

Every evening, pleasure cruises on the Mandovi River are available, offering music, singing and dancing; there is, of course, also a small bar on board. The one-hour "Sunset Cruise" is perfect for the romantic at heart: the glowing red sun disappears into the Arabian Sea beyond the Mandovi delta accompanied by Portuguese and Indian folk dances and melancholy folk songs, reminiscent of the "Fado" in Lisbon. Departures at 6 and 7 pm; price: 35 Rs. The two-hour tour aboard the "Sta. Monica" includes a Goan dinner. Departures at 7 and 9 pm; price: 50 Rs. For moon-struck romantics, there are special evening cruises when the moon is full; price: 50 Rs., information on departure times upon request. A number of ships can be rented for private celebrations and tours from the Manager of the Travel Division in the Tourist Hotel. An air conditioned "luxury launch" for 150 passengers costs 2000 Rs. for the first hour; each additional hour, 600 Rs. Without air conditioning, the price for a charter boat accommodating 150 passengers falls to 1700 Rs. for the first hour and 300 Rs. per additional hour. The base price for a "luxury launch" for 70 passengers is around 850 Rs.; each additional hour is charged at 300 Rs.

Trained, state-certified tour guides can also be hired through the Tourist Information Office in the Tourist Hotel. Prices range from 35 to 80 Rs. per day, depending on group size; a set surcharge of 25 Rs. is added to the price for tours given in languages other than English.

Gurudwara

Almost one percent of the Goans are Sikhs. The founder of their religion, Guru Nanak (1496 — 1538), the first of ten gurus, integrated Hindu and Islam beliefs into a new religion. The basis of the Sikh faith is contained in the ''Granth Sahib,'' the holy book. In their ''Gurudwaras,'' usually whitewashed Sikh houses of worship, they meet shortly before dark for a collective religious service. The only two Sikh houses of worship were built on Mangor Hill in Vasco da Gama and in Betim.

Harmal/Harbal →*Arambol*

History

The Beginning of a Legend

''He always returned to the ledge on the red cliffs for three weeks and gazed out over the sea. Brahma had finally given him enlightenment. The divine Pasuram drew his bow and shot an arrow out into the sea. Then a mighty storm divided the water and a fertile strip of land covered with coconut trees, gentle mountain slopes, rivers and plains graced with flowers emerged from the sea: Goa.'' (From the Mahabharata)

The ancient Hindu scriptures and legends, like the Mahabharata, refer to this narrow strip of coastline inhabited by the legendary people of Gomantah as ''Gopakattam,'' ''Govapuri'' and ''Gomant.'' The official history begins in 300 B.C. At that time, Goa was a part of the Moorish Empire. At the time of Christ's birth, the Satavahanas from Kolhapur ruled the land, followed by the reign of the Chalukyan Dynasty from Badami (580 to 750 A.D.). They were driven out by the beginning of the 11th century by the Kadamba kings, who founded a settlement for the first time in Goa's history. Their capital Chandrapura, later named ''Govopuri,'' lay on the banks of the Zuari River. Around 1312, Bahamani

A view from one of the many beach resorts on Colva Beach ▶

Moslems conquered the city and ruled for 58 years until their main trade partner, the powerful kingdom of Vijayanar, under the rule of Harihara I, annexed Goa in 1370. Under the rule of the Vijayanar kings, peace reigned for a hundred years in Goa. However, in 1470, the Bahamani Moslems under the leadership of Mahmud Gavan demanded back the fertile strip of coastline. They founded their capital city of Elo on the Mandovi River, on the site where Old Goa stands today. In 1482, Yusuf Adil Shah of Bijapur with his troops conquered the small trade settlement and developed it into a capital city.

Canons, Churches and Commerce

December 19, 1961: Only 14 years after the fruitless attempt to annex Goa into the young Indian nation through diplomatic channels, president Jawaharlal Nehru ordered 30,000 Indian soldiers to assemble against the Portuguese troops which numbered only 3000. The Indian Armada, trained under the direction of Great Britain and equipped with Soviet weaponry, fought at sea against the completely antiquated Portuguese sloops, and on land against the war-weary mercenaries of a decaying colonial power. The military mission "fly-swatter" took the unprepared Portuguese colonial lords completely by surprise. Goa, together with its two northern strongholds Daman and Diu in Gujarat, were consequently integrated as territories of the Indian Republic. Nehru needed this domestic political triumph to offset his foreign policy which foresaw a possible war with China. However, Portugal was not willing to give up its "Goa Dourada," its Golden Goa, quite so quickly, despite their defeat: Lisbon maintained an exile government for 13 years. It was only with the "Revolution of Carnations" that the requisites were established for a reinstatement of diplomatic relations between Delhi and Lisbon.

The city on the banks of the Tejo had controlled the course of Goa's history for 451 years. For a short time, Lisbon was the largest commercial centre under the sun, securing an impressive title for its monarch Manuel I: "King of Portugal and the Algarve, Master of Navigation and Conqueror of Ethiopia, Persia and India." The preconditions for Portugal's almost legendary climb to power were establish over one hundred years earlier by Henry the Mariner. With the introduction of the compass to navigation and the creation of more manoeuvrable sailing vessels, the caravel, which could also be steered against the wind, thus staying on course, Henry had created the necessary nautical basis for extensive expeditions. Economically, the slave trade held great promise of lucrative profits. The merchant family Fugger from Augsburg also presented problems for young prince Henry, who was hopelessly far from the

throne in terms of succession — through their monopoly, this family controlled the entire European market for luxury goods such as silk, jade and spices.
In 1497, a man appeared on the political scene, whose name is now also that of the second largest city in Goa: Vasco da Gama. The military commander and diplomat set sail in that same year with four ships and a crew of 140 to locate a sea passage to India. Prior to this, the treaty of Tordesillas had apportioned the western hemisphere to Spain; the eastern, to Portugal. Ten years after Bartolomeu Dia's fruitless attempt, Vasco da Gama sailed by the Portuguese trading posts along the coast of West Africa, safely traversed the Cape of Good Hope, passed Mosambique and came upon Arab merchants in Mombasa. Their reception was hostile. Thus, Vasco da Gama continued onto Malindi, where he met Ahmed Ibn Majid, an experienced navigator who lead Vasco da Gama's fleets as the helmsman to Calicut on India's Malabar Coast, about 3,000 kilometres south of Goa.

Upon his first landing, Vasco da Gama was not successful in seizing the trading settlement and founding a Portuguese merchant colony. He requested help from the king, and with that, a fleet of 13 ships equipped with cannons and 1200 heavily armed soldiers set sail for Calicut under the command of Pedro Alvares Cabral. While Vasco da Gama's fleets had already begun the voyage home, Cabral was able, using military pressure, to found a trading colony. Any opposition was bloodily quashed. 800 Arabs were beheaded. Before his departure, Cabral set fire to the city.

In 1502, Vasco da Gama set off on his second journey. The events that followed proved that Cabral's brutality was only a foretaste of what was to come. The Portuguese would stop at nothing to destroy the Arab, Persian and Turkish trade links. Vasco da Gama pillaged and sunk all of the Arabian ships in the harbour. The crews were driven through the city, their hands and ears cut off, to force the Arabian Emperor Raja to order the retreat of the Arabs.

In 1510, a new phase in Portuguese colonial politics began. Alfonso de Albuquerque, the man with the clearest concepts for the future of the new overseas territories, became the king's most respected and trusted advisor. He suggested that a network of fixed trading outposts be established, which would then be guarded by armed troops. To ensure the protection of the forts, it was also planned to trade with the inhabitants. Penetration into the country's interior in the sense of colonial occupation was not (yet) intended. Albuquerque later found his stronghold in what later became Goa Velha, at that time still only a small trade colony about 12 kilometres up the Mandovi River. It had been founded in 1480 by Arabs with trade relations to the neighbouring kingdoms of Bijapur and Vijayanagar. The advantage of Goa's location were obvious:

the close proximity of the Westghats, with their expansive teak forests facilitated the building and repair of ships; in addition, the colony already had a well-developed and easily defended harbour. Albuquerque landed in Goa with 25 caravels in 1510. His 60,000 soldiers killed or drove out the 7,000 resident Moslems in a matter of a few days. The new fortifications were quickly erected. Albuquerque had the existing palace enlarged to include a hospital and a mint. The Portuguese king's absolute claim to power was further emphasised with the laying of the cornerstones for numerous churches. The new settlement blossomed at once. The population already numbered 250,000 in 1565. The cities riches were a result of the trade with the kingdom of Vijayanagar, located about 350 kilometres away in what is now the state of Karnataka. This kingdom was in need of horses for the battle against the Moghuls who were invading from northern India. The demand was appropriately high considering the tropical climate and the number of battles. Furthermore, Goa was the definitive centre of trade with southeast Asia, where the Portuguese also maintained trading posts in Canton, Malacca and Macao among other locations.
The new rulers exercised little restraint in regard to the lives of the natives. At first religious tolerance was practised. Only the burning of widows was forbidden. This ritual, called ''sati,'' was first banned by the English in 1875. Cooperation instead of confrontation was the motto. The high taxes under Arab rule were lowered and Indians were involved in the administration of the new state. The essential goal of the colonial politics included plans for an increase in the population. Because the home country of Portugal had a population of less than one million, there was often a shortage of people: Portugal's fields often remained uncultivated because many sought quick riches through trade with India. Countless people died during the crossing or of tropical diseases. Thus, Albuquerque asserted his plans to allow interracial marriages between his sailors and Indian women, against the will of the church. Even Portuguese orphans were brought to Goa to be married to Indian women who had been converted to Christianity. If Goan boys lost their fathers, they were educated in the monastery. Goa's economic-worldly colonisation went hand in hand with its religious subordination: the church made its claim to power in regard to the intensive missionary work. Dominicans were already on the first ships leaving for Goa. The Franciscans followed in 1517 and only 20 years later did the most important order, the Jesuits lead by Francis Xavier, appear on the scene. The church viewed fighting ignorance and illiteracy as the most effective instruments in converting the heathens. Countless local schools and a reputable university were founded. In 1514, a theological seminary would follow. Here, the Indians received a theological education but could not be ordained. The

religious tolerance gave way to the nightmare of the Inquisition under the pressure of the counter-reformation. The caste system was abolished and the Indians were not allowed to practice their religion. In 1567, all of the Hindu temples were destroyed and, as a sign of the new rulers' might, ostentatious churches were built in their place.

In 1580, the Spanish monarch Philip I annexed Portugal. Thus, Goa became a Spanish territory up until 1640. Even today, the coat of arms over the Santa Monica Convent in Old Goa remains as evidence of the sixty years of Spanish rule, which brought incredible advances to the colony.

The end of the Spanish rule was brought about by the terrible invasion of the Dutch. The Portuguese then answered this attack with as much blood as in Cabral: all of the Dutch merchants were hung. Another attack from the sea directed toward Fort Aguada, built in 1612 at the mouth of the Mandovi River, was also successfully averted. Chochin and other small spice harbours, however, fell into the hands of the new adversaries. As was formerly the case with the caravels, the superiority of the Dutch marine forces was decisive: now it was the Dutch who had the more manoeuvrable ships equipped with a larger number of cannons. Holland drove the Portuguese out of Ceylon (1609), but fell into bitter conflict with the English. The East Indian Company, the supporter of the English colonial policy, was no longer content with mere bases, but organised and planned the deliberate and profit-oriented colonisation of the Indian subcontinent. The centres of the Indo-British Empire arose over one hundred years after Albuquerque's territorial annexations in Goa: Madras (1639), Bombay (1661), Calcutta (1696).

During that time, Goa sank into a sort of lethargy, to then awaken under the administration of Pont (1750 -1777). The Goan "Renaissance" was predominantly intellectual in nature. The Portuguese could compete neither economically nor militarily with the Dutch, English and French in the international arena. During the early 18th century, a malaria epidemic broke out in the capital, Goa Velha. Around 10% of the population succumbed to this disease. With the spread of the malaria epidemic, the capital was moved up the river to Panjim, which, from thie time on, would be called Nova Goa. Old Goa, deserted and reduced to insignificance, was quickly overgrown by the stifling tropical vegetation. All traces of the houses of the former residence have completely disappeared, only the churches have endured.

A vivid figure of that time was the Abbot José Faria. When his liberal movement striving for Goan autonomy once again threatened to jeopardise the Portuguese rule, the politically unpleasant abbot was sent to Portugal without hesitation, where he was destined to have difficulties with the Inquisition. The

abbot's fame was less a result of the statue in Panjim than of his adventurous escape through France. The author Alexandre Dumas immortalised the abbot imprisoned in the Château d'If, in *The Count of Monte Christo.*
Under the pretence of the Napoleonic Wars, the English occupied Goa from 1800 — 1802 and 1808 — 1813. In 1836, London presented a proposal to purchase Goa: The Britons offered 200,000 Pounds Sterling for the Lusitanian enclave — however, the Portuguese explicitly refused. Thus, it was left to the irony of history that Goa was to emerge from the foreign rule as the only remaining as well as oldest colony in India. After the English paved the way for the founding of the Indian Union on August 15, 1947 with their military withdrawal, Nehru was not successful in securing Goa, Daman and Diu through diplomatic channels. The Goan "liberation" came only after 451 years, in 1961.

Parting with Paradise?

Hardly liberated, the new "invaders" were already standing on the threshold: During the mid 1960's, Goa became a Mecca for hippies and social nonconformists. Sex, drugs and rock'n'roll determined the lives of these flower children. At first, curiously ogled by the natives, and later tolerated, they lived secluded in their grass huts and their small, Mediterranean-style houses, threw their beach parties and lead an alternative lifestyle far away from the conventions of European civilisation. The peaceful invasion from the west gave way to the organised mass-tourism of the mid 1980's. This development lead the small state into a vicious circle of dependence: the economic boom destroyed Goa's natural resources. For instance the water supply: both in 1987 and 1988, the monsoon did not occur. In desperation, the populace fought over the last remaining drops of water, while the larger hotel complexes watered their grass regularly, cleaned their swimming pools daily and refilled them with fresh water. The water table, which was stable at 22 metres up until the mid 1980's, continues to sink alarmingly since the beginning of the tourist boom. The same is true for electricity: the feeble power supply is hopelessly overburdened by the hotel complexes. Power failures and dark cities at night have become routine in Goa.
Opposition is crystallising. Professor Sergio Carvalho was ethically appalled at the "moral decay through the fat, slovenly and often naked Europeans," as quoted in an interview in the local newspaper "The Navhind Times" in November 1987. He initiated a devout civil protest movement. Members of Carvalho's "Jagrut Goencaranchi Fauj" (JGF) greeted the passengers of the first charter flight to land in Dabolim on November 7, 1987 with a deluge of rotten

eggs, tomatoes and fish tails. As a precaution, before the arrival of the second charter plane on November 14, 1987, JGF leader Carvalho and two of his followers Roland Martin and Rodney Pereira were placed in police custody. For two weeks, all hotels were guarded by the police. Armed soldiers in combat uniforms escorted all shuttle and tour buses. Hotel guests were asked to stay within the hotel complexes. Meanwhile, the situation has returned to normal by western standards. The abundance of money from the tourists has spurred inflation; drugs have fastened their grip on even the Goan young people, bringing an increase in crime: the previously typical petty crimes consisting of theft and misdemeanours resulting from vague legal interpretations have given way to robbery, murder and rape. Calangute now ranks with Miami Beach. In Goa's interior, where the traditional Goa has sought refuge, every measure is taken to keep the beach's tourists at bay. It's better to have a few less Rupees than naked strangers, is their motto. A deep rift has developed between the sun-hungry Europeans and Indian honeymooners on the one hand, and the Goan residents on the other.

Holiday Apartments →*Accommodation*

Holidays and Celebrations

There are so many festivals and celebrations in Goa that there is always some special event going on nearby, no matter where one might be in Goa. Because the Hindus and Moslems divide the year according to lunar cycles or the Moslem calendar, their festivals are on different days each year.

While many of the festivals celebrated by the residents in the individual villages are in honour of local deities, the two largest Hindu festivals put the entire region of Goa into a religious rapture. The mass onset of pious Hindus, who surrender to religious abandon in honour of the gods, leads to a number of deaths each year.

Shigmo: The India Holi festival is called "shigmo" in Goa. Bonfires are lit in celebration of the beginning of spring and the coming of the vital monsoon rains. Brightly coloured powders and coloured water are sprinkled on people, animals and buildings, symbolizing the exuberant spectrum of colour of the tropical springtime.

Diwali: The most merry and exuberant Hindu festival takes place during five days in November. The "Festival of Lights," also in November, marks the beginning of a new fiscal year. Every evening, countless lights, candles and oil lamps are lit all over Goa; fireworks explode against the backdrop of the night sky. The religious background of ''Diwali" are the sacrificial ceremonies in honour of the goddesses Kali and Lakshmi, the two female incarnations of Shiva and Vishnu.

The most significant holidays and celebrations in Goa include:

Christian Holidays

January 6: Epiphany in Chandor, Cansaulim and Reis Magos
February 2: ''Our Lady in Candelaria" church celebration; Pompurpa
February/March: Carnival in all of Goa
Fifth Monday in Lent: All Saint's Procession of the Third Order of St. Francis; Old Goa
First Sunday after Easter: Festival of Jesus of Nazareth; Siridao
16 days after Easter: ''Our Lady of Miracles" Festival; Mapusa
August 24: Festival de Novidades (the first bundles of rice are ceremonially presented to the head of state).
October 1 to 14: Fama de Menino Jesus (in honour of the Christ child); Colva
Third Wednesday in November: ''Our Lady in the Rosary" Festival; Navelim
December 3: Festival commemorating the anniversary of St. Francis Xavier's death; Old Goa
December 8: ''Our Lady of Immaculate Conception" Festival; Panjim
December 25: Christmas
December 31: New Year's Eve

Public Holidays

January 26: Republic Day
August 15: Independence Day
October 2: Mahatma Gandhi's Birthday

Moslem Holiday

Zilhaj (February) 17: Festival (Urus) of Shah Abdullah; Panjim

Hindu Holidays

March: Ramnathi: Kavlem, Mangueshi, Ponda, Shiroda, Brahmapuri
Shigmo: Kasarpal, Phatarpa, Cuncolim, Panjim
Gudi Pawda (Hindu New Year): in all of Goa
April: Rangapanchami: Kasarpal, Zambaulim, Quepem
Ramnavi: Partagal-Canacona
Chaitra Purnima: Borim, Nangueshi, Chandranath, Ponda, Sanquelim, Quepem
May: Fire-walking: Sirigao-Assonora

The various gods of India are often portrayed erotically ▶

July: Saplaha: Vasco
August: Gokul Asthami: Narvem, Bicholim
September: Ganesh Chaturti: in all of Goa
October: Dasrotsav: Pernem
Navrata Utsav: in all Hindu temples; ten-day festival commemorating the victory of Rama over the demon Ravana (also called ''Dussehra")
November: Diwali: in all of Goa; Festival of Lights in honour of the goddess Lakshmi, Hindu New Year
December: Dattajyanti: Sanquelim

Hospitals →*Medical Care*
Hotels →*Accommodation*
Identification →*Travel Documents*

Information

In the US: Information Service of India, 3 East 64th Street, New York, NY 10021-7097 (In the General Consulate)
In other countries →*Travel Documents, individual Embassies*
In Goa →*Tourist Information*

Insurance in Case of Illness

The health care system in Goa is sufficient in terms of Goa's needs and is — in comparison to the average Indian standard — quite exceptional. Panjim is the centre of the health care system with its renowned Medical College and numerous private and public clinics *(→Panjim).* All of the common medications are available in Goa with no problems. However, those who require certain medications on a regular basis should have sufficient supplies prescribed by a doctor in their home country. Serious tropical diseases like Malaria and Filaria (nematodes) have been eliminated. Those who wish to take no chances can take out a comprehensive insurance policy, usually available through travel agents, including, in addition to luggage insurance, health and accident coverage. →*Medical Care*

Kansarpal

Kansarpal is 14 kilometres northeast of Mapusa, located in the Bicholim province.

Worth seeing is the **Shri Kalikadevi Temple:** This temple is presumed to be about 800 years old and is dedicated to the goddess Kali, the demonic and destructive side of the goddess Durga.

Kawale (Quela)

The town of Kawale with its population of almost 7,000 is located about 2.5 kilometres west of Ponda. The religious centres of the "smartas" or "shaivas," the followers of Shiva, are found here. In the monastic school Kaivalyapur Matha, young Brahmans are trained as priests.

Kawale / **Sights**

Shantadurga Temple: This temple was built during the mid 18th century on the site where, according to local mythology, Shantadurga appeared in the form of a messenger of peace, to settle a conflict between Shiva and Vishnu. The statue of the goddess stands between the two rival deities.

Language

Over 200 dialects and 17 recognised languages make for a linguistic jumble in India, intensified through the forms of speech used within individual families and clans. Thus, English still remains the leading official language. Besides English, there are two other equally recognised official languages: Hindi, the most commonly spoken language in northern India; and Tamil, spoken in the southern states of the Indian Union. Despite its size, Goa is characterised by a multiplicity of languages. With the recognition of the locally spoken Konkani language as the official language, Goa was able to free itself from the status of a territory under the authority of the Hindu government in Delhi and become an independent state in the union in January, 1987. Almost 90% of the population are native speakers of the official Konkani language, the only Indian language with Latin letters. In addition, English and Hindi share equal status as official languages in Goa. 3% of the population stated Portuguese as their native language in the census in 1981. Foreign workers from the north often speak Marathi, the official language in the powerful neighbouring state of Maharashtra, while newcomers from Karnataka speak Kanada, also called Karnath.

In the large hotel complexes, tourists should have no problems communicating: perfect English is required of hotel employees. They do, however, remain true to their local language when greeting guests. They will put the palms of their hands together and greet guests with a slight bow and say ''namaste" — welcome.

Maps

Maps which include only the Goa region are a scarce commodity. Usually, these cannot be purchased separately, but are included in Goan travel guides. The best option is to request the free map with a scale of 1:200,000 from the Tourist Information Office. On the reverse side of the map, next to the city map of Panjim are also the most important sights, beaches, accommodation and general information. More general maps of southern India are less useful because Goa appears on them as only a tiny spot, which makes planning tours and trips nearly impossible.

→*Travel Literature*

Mapusa (Mapuca)

The capital of the Bardez province with a population of over 30,000 is located 13 kilometres north of Panjim and is the economic centre of northern Goa. The city, which is called ''Mapsa" for short in the local dialect, offers no sights worth mentioning. Only the weekly market on Fridays, known for its inexpensive fashions, is worth strolling through.

Mapusa / **Practical Information**

Accommodation: *I. Western Standards*

Satyahara Hotel, Tel: 28 49, air conditioned, TV.

Hotel Bardez, Tel: 26 07.

Tourist Hotel, on the traffic junction / entrance to the city in the direction of Anjuna.

II. Indian Style

Hotel Safari, across from the Mamlatdar's Office.

Janki Shankar Lodge, Kareka Building, Tel: 4 01, simple double rooms.

Hospital: Tel: 23 72

Pharmacies: Cosme Matias Menezes, near the city hall, Tel: 2 78; Menezes & Cia., near the city hall, Tel: 1 43; Union Pharmacy, near the bus station; Joao Menezes Pharmacy, on the marketplace; Drogeria Colvakar, near the city hall, Tel: 3 22.

Police: Tel: 22 31
Restaurants: Imperial Bar & Restaurant: clean, predominantly local clientele. Tourist Hotel: large public dining hall.
Transportation: Mapusa is a junction point for transportation in northern Goa. The buses run mainly according to demand, meaning without a set schedule. The shuttle busses to Vagator and Anjuna are especially overflowing with western backpack tourists, who will not entrust their luggage to the roof rack on the bus. The buses do not run after 8 pm.

Margao (Madgaon)

Margao, the second largest city in Goa with around 50,000 residents, is situated 33 kilometres south of Panjim in the middle of Salcete, Goa's rice belt. Even before the Portuguese took over Goa, this city near the Sal River was a thriving centre for trade and commerce. The legends report that during the Aryan settlement of the land around 3000 B.C., agriculture was already practised in this region. During the colonial rule, many landowners settled with their families in this provincial capital.

Margao / **Sights**

Holy Ghost Church: Archbishop Dom Gaspar de Pereira commissioned the construction of this municipal church in 1565 on the foundation of the demolished main Hindu temple. However, the rage resulting from the foreign "Christian" dominance was so intense that Hindus and Moslems joined forces to burn down the ostentatious church only a few years later. The vengeful arson was futile: the baroque church with its lavish decor built in its place in 1589 was a manifestation of the Portuguese power.
The villas of the high nobility on the large square in front of the Church of the Holy Ghost (all 200 to 300 years old) awaken the recollection of the golden age of the Portuguese crown colony. The church's square is used by the pupils from the neighbouring girls' school, run by the nuns from the Holy Ghost Convent, for sports practice. The girls practice javelin throwing and gymnastics here in their white and blue school uniforms.
Aga Khan Park: In the centremost part of the city, the city park offers welcome relief from the dust and noise of the Indian cities. Adjacent to a small children's playground with imaginative wooden equipment is a well-groomed greenbelt, in which an abundance of tropical flowers dots the meadows with bright points of colour.

To the right and left of Station Road, behind the **Municipal Building** is the area where the old marketplace, **Mercado Vasco da Gama,** and the new marketplace, **Mercado Alfonso de Albuquerque,** are set up — the largest and probably most lovely **market** in Goa. Those looking to investigate the markets will certainly get their money's worth.

Margao / **Practical Information**

Accommodation: *I. Western Style*

Hotel Metropole, Avenida Concessao, Tel: 31 69 and 34 05, two restaurants, bar, discotheque, roof garden, book store.

Hotel Sal, Rua Martires, near the Hari Mandir, Tel: 23 79.

Hotel Mabai, at the upper end of the Municipal Gardens, Tel: 36 53/4/5, restaurant, bar, roof garden.

Hotel Woodlands, Tel: 31 21.

Tourist Hotel, near the marketplace.

II. Indian Style

Government Rest House, Monte Hill, Tel: 29 96.

Carolina Hotel, near the Cine Lata.

Durga Hotel, Khanbard Road, Tel: 23 06.

Goa Guest House, near the railway crossing, Tel: 22 57.

Gokula Hotel, behind the Grah Church, Tel: 31 18.

Hotel Bambino, Fr. Miranda Road, Tel: 31 34.

Hotel Paradri, across from the Milan Hotel.

Royal Hotel, near the Bank of Baroda, Tel: 22 03.

Hotel Three Star, Road Madla Bazar.

Hotel Naaz, Khareband Road, Tel: 32 01.

Automobile Repairs: Narcinva D. Nalk, Tel: 2 11 43; Virgincar & Sons, Tel: 2 27 71; Jose Francisco dos Santos, Vidyanagar, Tel: 2 06 59.

Hospital: Tel: 2 21 64.

Information: Tourist Information Centre, City Hall, Tel: 25 13.

Night Life: Hotel Sal Restaurant, ''Cabaret Show,'' daily, except Mondays, Tel: 23 79.

Pharmacies: Cosme Matias Menezes, across from the city hall, Tel: 22 14; Menezes & Cia., Marketplace, Tel: 21 18; Farmacia Salcete, Tel: 21 68; Drogeria Prakash, Lotlikar Building, Tel: 24 89; Hindu Pharmacy, near the Govind Buildings, Tel: 28 29.

Police: Tel: 2 21 75

Restaurants: Hotel Sal Restaurant, Tel: 23 79
Shalimar Cellar, next to the taxi stand
Longuinhos Restaurant, next to the Municipality
Venice Restaurant, Loiha Maidan
Nevette Restaurant, next to the taxi stand
Train Station: Tel: 2 22 52
Transportation: Shuttle buses run hourly to Colva via Benaulim, then further south to Betul. Travel time: 30 minutes to Colva, a little over an hour to Betul. The route to Panjim is one of the most beautiful in Goa, the trip lasts one and a half hours. The view from the middle of the Zuari Bridge is especially impressive.
Travel Agencies: Goa Travel Service, Vit-Rose Mansion, Isidoro Baptista Road; Suvina Travels, Gosalia Building, Tel: 32 52; Rau Raje Desprabhu, Tel: 24 40.

Margao / **Surroundings**

The periphery of the provincial capital offers several interesting sights:
Rachol Seminary: About three kilometres from the small town of Raia is the architecturally interesting Rachol Seminary with its church dating back to the 17th century. The interior includes some remarkable religious frescoes.
Also worth seeing is the old library, which is meanwhile no longer in use. Earlier, this library ranked among the best in Goa. The Rachol Seminary houses one of the few Protestant schools in Goa.
Christ Ashram Exorcist Centre: East of the road from Margao to Cortalim, near the town of Nuvem, genuine Catholic exorcisms take place in a Hindu ambience. The number of cases is enormous: daily, a long line waits in front of the gates — usually women and young girls in saris, who were sent to have the inane chatter driven out of them.

Markets

In almost every town, markets take place from once to several times a week — everything is sold here from plastic buckets to pickled fish, from papayas to saris.

Mayem

Mayem is a small town on the shore of Mayem Lake, located in the Bicholim province. Its idyllic location among the rolling green hills makes the lake a popular picnic spot for local residents and holiday travellers alike.

Accommodation: Mayem Lake Resort, Tel: Bicholim 94 (Reservation Authority Caretaker).

Mayem / **Surroundings**

Shri Sapta Koteshwar Temple: located near Narve. It was especially the Kadamaba kings who worshipped the goddess of this temple. Originally this sacred building was situated on Diwadi Island. After the Portuguese destroyed it, the deity was brought to its present location. In 1688, Chatrapati Shivaji drove the Portuguese from the small town and had the temple rebuilt. The lingam with its various facets is venerated as ''dharlinga.“

Medical Care

International health insurance vouchers are not accepted in India. In case of illness, the hotel reception will contact a physician (often there is one on the premises) who can refer a patient to the hospital in Panjim if need be. The medical college is also in Panjim. The doctors' fees in India are far below those common, for example, in European countries. Because the invoices must be paid right away, it is definitely necessary, for insurance reasons, that these include a detailed description of the treatment and any medications given. There is no general vaccination obligation. A vaccination for yellow fever is, however, obligatory for travellers who were recently in an infected area. A malaria prophylactic can definitely be recommended. Apparently, Goan malaria have developed a resistance to Cloroquine compounds; therefore, one should combine these with another prophylactic. Current information is available through tropical disease centres. After returning to your home country, the malaria treatment must be continued due to malaria's long incubation period. It is also advisable to be inoculated for tetanus, typhus and cholera. Any medication that might be needed will be available in Goa.

Medications that one should bring along include any prescription medications, charcoal tablets for diarrhoea and a disinfectant for minor injuries. Also bring enough suntan lotion with a high protection factor as well as a small bottle of insect repellent.

Medication →*Medical Care*

Molem National Park

Also called "Bhagwan Mahaveer Sanctuary," this, the largest national park in Goa, extends along Goa's northernmost border to Karnataka, encompassing 240 square kilometres and ascending to an altitude of over 800 metres at the base of the Westghats. This wildlife and nature reserve starts at the entrance to the town of Molem near the Tourist Centre. The Tourist Centre also offers simple, clean and inexpensive accommodation.

Setting one's expectations too high in regard to observing the wildlife can lead to disappointment because poachers continually pillaged this park up until 1972. The wildlife has recovered to a certain extent. The reserve is home to jackals, pythons, king cobras, sloth bears and hundreds of apes. The local residents believe that in addition to the 80 Gaurs (a type of Bison), an occasional panther also prowls through the undergrowth.

The mountain forest, its foliage increasing with its altitude, is especially interesting. The view from the panorama road, the national thoroughfare to Karnataka, at an altitude of 600 metres above bamboo thickets, fresh with ivy,

The lush green of a betel nut plantation near Aldona

vine-draped trees and exotic flowers on the slopes leading down to the flatlands is simply breathtaking.

Since 1987, tours of the park and guided hikes to observatory platforms (machan) are offered. By no means should one attempt to climb the observation posts on one's own.

Information: Park Office (next to the Forest Rest House)

Accommodation: Forest Rest House, Tourist Cottages

Money →*Currency*

Mormugao

Near the mouth of the Zuari River, not far from Vasco da Gama, lies Goa's main transshipment harbour for arriving and departing ships: Mormugao. This natural harbour, protected by the monsoon winds by its location, is Goa's only harbour which is in operation during the entire year.

Through British support in planning and financing, it was made possible to expand this, Goa's main harbour, according to international standards. The harbour is also the largest employer in Vasco and provides work for numerous visiting labourers from the neighbouring Indian states. When the wharf workers striked for higher wages in 1987, a strike lasting several weeks, this also led to the downfall of the Goan government. Mormugao is simultaneously Goa's Naval base.

Worth seeing is **Fort Mormugao.** Built in 1624 to protect the, at that time, small harbour, this fort was enlarged extensively later in the 19th century.

Museums

* Old Goa: Archaeological Museum and Portrait Gallery, in the Monastery of St. Francis of Assisi, Tel: 59 41. Open 10 am to noon and 1 to 5 pm; closed Fridays.

* Panjim: Museum of Goa, Daman & Diu / Historical Archive, Ashirwar Building, 1st Floor, Santa Inez, Tel: 60 06. Open 9:30 am to 1 pm and 2 to 5:30 pm; closed Saturdays, Sundays and on public holidays. Galleria Esperanza (across from the Merces Church), Vodi Merces. Open 9 am to noon and 2 to 6 pm; making an appointment in advance is recommended.

Music

Music is inseparable from the Goan lifestyle. While mostly Mediterranean sounding melodies can be heard from open windows, Portuguese music dominates the older parts of the cities, and native Goans can often be seen on the beaches playing guitar or mandolin. The classic Indian music has no traditional roots in Goa. Even the increasing number of Indians who settle in Goa from other parts of India can not change this fact: the young people bring American pop music to Goa rather than traditional ragas or sitar music.

''Mandos,'' lyrical love songs, rank among the most popular type of music. The ''fados'' have sadder sounding melodies, characterised by a melancholy mood. These developed in the old quarters of Lisbon over 500 years ago, and remain in their original form in Goa today. Those interested in hearing this type of music should buy the cassette ''Goa — meu amor'' by Orlando and his Folklorists in the local record shop. While the most popular Portuguese folk songs are recorded on the A-side, the B-side presents original folk music in Konkani. The vocalists recorded on this cassette — Annette Pinto, Cynthia Largo Afonso, Shramila Colaco and June D'Gracias — rank among the most famous voices in Goa. They have all produced solo albums.

Goa's multicultural climate is an excellent environment for pop musicians, whose popularity extends beyond Goa's borders. Remo, Goa's premier pop star, repeatedly achieved high ratings at the ''Grand Prix d'Eurovision'' with his compositions interpreted by German and French artists. On the cassette ''Old Goa Gold,'' Remo interprets classic folk songs in Portuguese and Konkani. His collection entitled ''Goan Crazy'' is in direct contrast, with its political sting.

Classical European music also enjoys good status in Goa. Every November, fans of classical music celebrate the ''Dirdi'' festival in Margao.

National Parks

Goa maintains three national parks to date, based on the guidelines of the ''Wild Animals and Birds Protection Act'' of 1968. The first marine preservation centre is under construction near Dona Paula. A major threat to the animals is personified by the poachers, who usually come from the neighbouring Indian states. They had managed to all but drain all three national parks of animals by 1970. Meanwhile, the animals have gradually recovered in numbers thanks to selective protective measures and high fines for poaching.

→*Bondla Wildlife Sanctuary*
→*Chorao Bird Sanctuary*

→Cotigao Wildlife Sanctuary
→Dona Paula
→Molem National Park

Nudity

As a rule: bathing topless or completely nude is prohibited in India and is offensive to the Indian sense of morals. Indian men have often only seen their own wives clothed in saris — even when fathering children. For this reason, the naked Europeans not only cause a civil uprising, but also the development of commercial voyeurism: hundreds of "pilgrims" flock to the beaches to catch a glimpse of the white women. Whoever swears by nudism despite all of this, should withdraw to the secluded niches on Arambol Beach and Baga Beach where nude bathing is tolerated. Whoever bathes nude in spite of the signs prohibiting this risks being reported to the police, and should expect a high fine. The beaches are constantly patrolled by policemen in street clothes — not only because of narcotics. The beaches are patrolled from boats along the coast as well.

Old Goa / Goa Vel(h)a

The history is the most interesting and colourful in Goa Vel(h)a, Old Goa, located about eight kilometres up the river on the southern banks of the Mandovi. This capital city of the Portuguese-Indian trade territory was already praised as "senhora de todo o Oriente" — the lady of the entire orient — by the famous Lusitanian bard, Luiz Vas de Camoes (1524 — 1580). There are more churches here within only one square kilometre than in Rome. Therefore, it is not surprising that the following saying developed: "Quem viu Goa, nao precisa ver Lisboa — whoever has seen Goa needs not see Lisbon." Other than the churches and monasteries, only an enormous cathedral remains of "Goa dourada," golden Goa. The residents' huts and houses have long since fallen victim to the monsoons and uncontrolled vegetation. To convince the "heathens" of the might and truth of Christian teachings, the victors built their gigantic houses of worship on the foundations of the intentionally destroyed Hindu temples and buildings in the small trade settlement of Adil Shah.

Old Goa / **Sights**

A visit to the church park in the jungle requires about half a day. A good starting point for an extensive tour through the impressive park is the deteriorating **Augustine Monetary,** today only a ruin, of which only the foundation and the 46-metre-high tower still stand. In 1587, 12 monks of the Augustine Order came to Goa. In 1602, they built this church, which ranked among the largest churches in the capital city. Its world-famous library drew intellectuals from all over the world — even scientists from Cambridge travelled here to conduct primary research. Because of the repressive politics of the Portuguese government, the Augustine monks gradually left Goa at the beginning of the 19th century. Seven years after giving up the diocese (1842), the arches had already collapsed. In 1931, the facade and half of a tower followed suit, and more parts of the church collapsed in consequent years.
Directly nearby is Goa's only convent, the **Santa Monica Convent,** in which a few Portuguese-speaking nuns still live according to the strict rules of the convent. This, the largest and oldest convent in all of south and east Asia,

Exotic: typical village with old Mediterranean-looking houses underneath palm trees

with enough room to accommodate 100 nuns, was built as a result of a power struggle between the Franciscan and Augustine monks. Later, this first convent in Asia submitted to the authority of the Augustine monks. The plot of land was bought for 3000 Pardaus and the laying of the corner stone took place on July 2, 1606. The construction had to be completed quickly, because on the 3rd of September, only two months later, the first nuns were to move in. These plans failed: it was only much later in 1627 that the convent was completed. Nine years later (1636), a devastating fire destroyed the three-storied building made from laterite rock. However, the reconstruction was already underway during the following year. The building which stands today was completed in 1637. Well into the 18th century, entrance into this convent was reserved exclusively for the Portuguese or descendants from Lusitanian-Indian families. It was finally a royal decree that suspended this restriction. The discrimination continued however: instead of the typical black veils, Indian nuns had to wear white veils and were required to pay a substantially higher dowry upon being accepted into the convent.

Above the portal, a coat of arms is hung in memory of Philipp I of Spain — since 1636, the convent stood under royal patronage. From the foyer, one can continue straight ahead to the cloisters, which are officially closed to visitors — a friendly request, however, is sometimes sufficient for a glance around the tranquil courtyard. On June 5, 1964, the ''Mater Dei Institute for Nuns" was opened in the Santa Monica Convent. 1,600 nuns of from the most diverse denominations and countries have been trained here for missionary work in their home countries.

To the left, a narrow hallway, in which red tiles and frescoes are presently being restored, leads to the **Santa Monica Church,** famous and reputed for its ''miraculous cross." During a procession on February 8, 1636, according to the stories told by the natives, the figure of the crucified Jesus is said to have repeatedly opened his eyes and moved his mouth as if to speak; blood is said to have flowed from the wounds from the crown of thorns and the nail wound in its back. This miracle repeated itself four days later — in the presence of the viceroy Dom Fr. Miguel Rangel and the entire congregation.

An asphalt street leads up the ''Monte Sacro," the sacred mountain to the oldest church in Goa: **Our Lady of the Rosary.** From the square in front of this church, there is a magnificent panorama including the Mandovi River, the rice fields in fresh shades of green; to the left, the nearby Arabian Sea, to the right, the foothills of the Westghats, which can reach an altitude of up to 1,022 metres. When Alfonso de Albuquerque (a Portuguese seafarer and viceroy of India) commanded the battle against the Sultan of Bijapur, conquering the small Arab trade settlement, he swore an oath: should he come out of the battle victorious, he would build a parish church on that very site. A small memorial plaque on the church's tower serves as a reminder of this promise. Our Lady of the Rosary is a skillful combination of local influence and the art of the renaissance: cashew, mango and pineapple motifs point to Goan stylistic influence, while the archways ornamented with Manuelian tiles evidence a European heritage. The white marble tombstone carved in the Gujarati style is a masterpiece of Indian sculpture.

On the way back down the asphalt road, the **Royal St. Anthony Chapel** with its impressive garden makes the short detour worthwhile. This chapel was built here in 1543 in honour of the national saint of Portugal. Like the neighbouring Santa Monica Convent, this chapel stood under royal patronage. It was closed in 1835 due to its state of disrepair, and was thoroughly restored in 1894 and 1961. In addition to the indigenous flowers and vegetables in the garden, more rare plants can also be found. To the right of the chapel is a yak-fruit tree. The pumpkin-like fruit is the heaviest type of bread-fruit in the world and can grow to the size of a medicine ball. Nearby, the poinsettias bloom in bright red during December. The banana groves near the exit bear smaller but more juicy fruit than is the case with the bananas in other parts of the western world. Those who try them here, however, will be mercilessly brought before court and tried as a thief. The nuns from the neighbouring convent accept no excuses.

St. John Convent: founded in 1685, the Order of St. John gave up the convent after their order was banned. Nine years later, this domicile became home to clergy from the Santa Monica Convent. After being restored in 1953, the Franciscans founded a home here for the elderly and handicapped.

Further down the road, one will come across the only church which was not whitewashed, but left unpainted: the **Bom Jesus Cathedral.** This church is dedicated to the Christ child. It's flat baroque facade of laterite and sandstone is remarkable. Bordering this church, built 1596 — 1602, is the **Jesuit Monastery** (completed in 1589). Today, it leaves a ghostly empty impression with its high rooms and long corridors. Earlier, however, the Jesuits rose to become the most powerful order, because the pope had charged them with missionary work. In 1759, the Jesuit Order was banned; the remaining orders of monks, in 1835. The property of these orders went to the state.

The most prominent Jesuit baptist and preacher was St. Francis from Basque, credited with the founding of churches as far away as Malacca, China and Japan. In the adjacent chapel dedicated to St. Francis Xavier, frescoes depict this monk's life and travels:

Francis Xavier, who counts as the most successful Christian missionary, was born in Fort Xavier in Navarro on April 7, 1504. At the age of 19, the young Basque nobleman began his studies in Paris. His academic achievements, however, remained modest; he enjoyed the diversion of the big city too much. Despite this, the time spent in Paris would become the decisive turning point in his life. There he met Ignatius of Loyola, with whom he would later plan the founding of the Jesuit Order. When the seven monks were finally able to win the recognition of the pope, Ignatius of Loyola convinced the rather skeptical and hesitant Francis Xavier to turn to missionary work. Thus, Francis Xavier, at age 35, boarded the "Santiago" and set sail for India in 1541. To his surprise, he found a large Christian congregation already in existence, living on the coast of Malabar: thirty thousand families, supposedly descendants of those Indians who were converted to Christianity by the apostle Thomas only two years after the crucifixion of Christ. It is, however, more probable that this was a larger group of Christians, which had immigrated to India from Mesopotamia. This would make Indian Christianity almost as old as the Roman. Even today, the members of this group are accordingly proud.

The dedicated missionary finally reached Goa in 1542. Appalled at the corrupt conditions which he found there, he wrote the following to King Manuel in Lisbon: "If you do not threaten your officials with the dungeon and confiscation of property for their avarice and indulgent lifestyles, then all of your orders to promote Christianity are in vain."

When the anticipated answer never came, Francis Xavier turned his back on the colony and put his energies toward the more successful missions. He spent three years with the pearl fishermen on the Koromandel coast in southeastern India. Then he moved on further east to the Moluccs. During his work — sometimes with up to 400 baptisms per day — he became friends with a Japanese, who took him to Sancian, a group of islands off the coast of China, in 1549. There, in his easternmost mission, he contracted pneumonia and died on December 3, 1552 at the age of 46, during the planning stages of a mission to China. But the well-deserved final peace would be postponed even longer. Directly after the saint's death, the odyssey of his remains began. First the body was buried on Sancian, then exhumed and transported to the Moluccs because the diocese there also had placed their claim on the bodily remains of the saint. Four years later, Francis Xavier's grave was opened once more — the corpse returned to Goa, where it was first provisionally stored in a crate in St. Paul's Collegium. It was only in 1613, over seventy years after his death, that Pope Gregory XV canonised Francis Xavier. The embalmed saint found his final, solemn resting place. In 1698, Cosimo II, Grand Duke of the Tuscany, donated the sarcophagus which stood in the chapel in the right wing of the church. The Florentine sculptor Giovani Batista Foggini worked for ten years on the sarcophagus. The intricate engravings of the silver shrine surrounding the sarcophagus is the work of a local artist (1636). Formerly, the shrine was ornamented with valuable jewels.

The corpse did not endure the constant movement very well — being stored in the cramped coffin literally broke his neck. In 1554, a deeply religious Portuguese woman bit off a toe to keep as a relic of Francis Xavier. While dragoonic penance was imposed upon the pious woman, the Jesuits cleaned the toe, consecrated it and placed it in a separate shrine which now stands in the hallway to the cloister. In 1615, part of a hand was hacked off and brought to the Jesuit church Chièsa S Gesù in Rome; four years later, the remaining part of the hand was sent to a Jesuit Seminary in Japan.

Every ten years (again in 1994), is the ceremonial opening of the coffin. Long lines of devout believers reverently pass by the coffin, cross themselves and place aromatic flower petals on the preserved corpse. The courageous even kiss the forehead of the saint. Every year on December 3, the anniversary of the death of St. Xavier, Old Goa is transformed into a colourful marketplace weeks prior to the event. Here, religion is only the motivation behind the teeming celebration of life. Thousands of pilgrims from every part of Goa and the neighbouring states bring the entire clan, lock stock and barrel, toting mountains of blankets, huge aluminium pots and pans filled with food prepared in advance, followed by pets and barnyard animals. They settle into the church's cloister, wash and fish in the nearby Mandovi and listen to the sermons that can be heard in every corner thanks to the "Francis Xavier Sound System." There are peddlers everywhere, praising the merits of what they happen to be selling at the time: bright plastic bracelets, cotton clothing, plastic canisters, stone rice mortars, knick-knacks and toys. Among the peddlers, one finds carts with roasted beans, chick-peas and peanuts. Other peddlers tempt the masses with bright yellow-orange, deep-fried pastries, still dripping with oil.

Across from the Bom Jesus Cathedral are (from the left): the St. Catherine Chapel, Church and Franciscan Monastery as well as the largest church in Goa, Sé Catédral.

St. Catherine's Chapel: Together with the Our Lady of the Rosary, the St. Catherine's Chapel is the oldest Christian house of worship in Goa. Alfonso de Albuquerque built this chapel in 1510 as a victory monument to celebrate the conquest of the city on St. Catherine's Day. A small plaque mounted in the wall next to the side door commemorates the addition of a wing, commissioned by George Cabral in 1550. In 1931, the Goan government added a further plaque in Portuguese marking the location of the gate to the vanquished Moslem city. St. Catherine's Chapel was built in the Renaissance architecture prevalent at that time. The chapel's unpretentious interior houses a simple altar with a statue of the Madonna.

The centre of the extensive missionary work undertaken by the Franciscans was the **Church of St. Francis of Assisi,** founded in 1517 by eight Franciscan monks and originally built only as a small chapel with three altars and choir chancels. After this original building was demolished, the church which stands today was built in its place in 1661. The church was thoroughly restored from 1762 — 1765. The old frescoes, painted in the European tradition, show scenes from the life of St. Francis; the ornamentation of the arches and walls are purely Hindu in origin. The basin for the holy water at the entrance to the church is a remnant of a column from a Hindu temple, destroyed during the siege in 1510. The floors deserve special attention — the family coat of arms on the grave slabs date back to the early 16th century. The main altar reminds the monks of their vows: poveritá, humilitá, obedienza — poverty, humility and obedience.

The former **Franciscan Monastery** now houses the **Archaeological Museum.** It was designed in 1964 by the Archaeological Survey of India. In front of the entrance, the bronze statue of Alfonso de Albuquerque, Goa's first governor up until 1513, gives an impression of how the powerful conquerors of Goa might have looked. The small collection includes portraits of various Portuguese viceroys, a model of a Portuguese caravel (medieval sailing vessel), which is unfortunately missing its rigging, and some cult engravings in stone from the Animist cult.

Measuring 86 by 56 metres, the **Sé Cathedral** is the largest religious building in Goa. Its construction was begun in 1562 under King Dom Sebastaio (1557 — 1578), lasting exactly one hundred years — until 1662. The Dominicans financed the lengthy and costly construction from the sale of royally owned land and treasure. The octagonal baptismal basin to the right of the entrance was carved from a single block of granite. Francis Xavier is said to have been baptised in this basin. To the left of the entrance, a gigantic fresco depicts St. Christopher — meanwhile no longer a saint — with young Jesus on his shoulders. The marble on the pillars was imported from Italy, quarried in Carrara. The main altar (1652) is dedicated to St. Katharina of Alexandria. This legendary martyr is one of the 14 patron saints, guardian of philosophers. Her symbols are the palm (signifying victory), the wheel of sharp knives and a book. Formerly, on St. Catherine's Day, there was a procession from St. Catherine's Chapel to the St. Catherine's Altar, where high mass was then held. Afterward, a huge festival was celebrated. The organ next to the main altar dates back to the 18th century. The entrance to the vestry is to the right of the main altar, with paintings depicting scenes from the life of St. Catherine. A model of St. Peter's Cathedral in Rome stands on the altar decorated in gold leaf. The condition of the 14 additional altars at the sides of the church varys greatly, but their restoration is already planned, being financed through the collections from the papal visit. Originally the facade had two towers; the northern tower collapsed on July 25, 1776, however. Located in the southern tower, in addition to four other bells, is the "Golden Bell," the largest bell in Goa. It was cast in the small town of Cuncolim and installed in the tower in 1652. During the Inquisition, it was rung at every Autodafé (heretic trial). The bell's stately name comes from a poem by Tomas Ribeiro: in "sino de ouro" he praises the bell for its unparalleled resonance. The Sé Cathedral is also Asia's only remaining building built in Manuelian architecture.

The **Archbishop's Palace** is to the northwest of the cathedral, an ostentatious residence which is occasionally still in use. Southwest of the palace is the prison with dungeons used during the Inquisition. Built in 1560, the use of this building was first prohibited in 1812. Today, there remain no traces of this building, in which exactly 16,172 executions were carried out between 1561 and 1774. The Inquisition's Autodafés were carried out outside the city walls at the Campo Lazaro. There is also a helicopter pad, surrounded by groves of palm trees and banana plantations. This was built for the papal visit in 1986. South of the inquisitor's prison was once the "Misericordia" with the Nossa Senhora de Serra Church. Albuquerque himself founded this church in fulfilment of a vow he made during his shipwreck; originally, he was also buried in this church. From there, the Rua Direita leads down to the riverbank and the Viceroy's Palace. The Viceroy's Archway, **Ribeira dos Vizereys,** spans the pier, from which an occasional boat departs for Panjim. Earlier, every viceroy entered the flourishing city through the archway which was formerly a part of the palace of the defeated Adil Shah. To the west was once the galley wharf, the Ribeira des Galés; to the east, the customs house and the grand bazaar. St. Catherine is depicted on the archway; surrendering to her, Yusuf Adil Shah, who was defeated by Albuquerque in 1510.

Of the **Viceroy's Palace,** acclaimed in early travel logs as the most magnificent building in the city, only the portal, built in Bijapur style, remains standing. The building began to decay with the relocation of the governmental residence in 1472, until its demolition in 1820. The laterite stones were transported to Panjim to be used in building houses there.

The main church of the Italian Theatian monks, **St. Kajetan,** ends the tour. Pope Urban III dispatched the Theatians in 1655 to bring Christianity to the kingdom of Golconda (near Hyderabad). When the monks were not granted entry there, they settled in Goa in 1640. Their church was built according to the original layout of St. Peter's Cathedral in Rome. The domes were replaced by two towers. The facade is made of red laterite covered with mortar. An inscription in large letters above the entrance reads: ''DOMUS MEA DOMUS ORATIONIS" (My house is a house of prayer). Today, the adjacent cloister is used as a seminary.

Those who have ample leisure time should also visit the following sights in Old Goa.

Along the road to Ponda is the Gateway to the St. Paul's Collegium, the Francis Xavier Chapel and up the hill to the left, the Church of Our Beloved Lady of the Mountain. The Church and Monastery of the Miraculous Cross is up the motorway exit toward Pilar. The old whipping post can be seen on the way to Neura. Finally, the Carmelite Church is located on the way to Kumbarjuva.

St. Paul's Collegium Gate: the gateway arch is all that remains of this once so famous Jesuit seminary. Opened in 1542, the seminary was built on the foundations of the destroyed Mosque in Adil Shah's Moslem trade settlement. For over 200 years, the Jesuits taught all of the theological sciences. Everyone was allowed entrance into the seminary regardless of nationality or religious belief. With the outbreak of the malaria epidemic in 1750, the Jesuits were forced to discontinue their teaching activities. They, however, did remain in the building until the government gave the order to tear it down in 1832 and to have the stones used in its construction transported to Panjim to be used in building houses there. The most famous teacher of the St. Paul's Collegium was Francis Xavier, who often held sermons in the adjacent church around 1544. The first printing press in India also stood in the St. Paul's Collegium. The Jesuit monks printed the first Indian edition of the ''Conclusiones Philosophicas."

St. Xavier Chapel: Not far from St. Paul's Collegium is the small building with a whitewashed mortar facade. When Francis Xavier was canonised in 1622, this chapel was dedicated to him. It served as a place of worship for the Collegium from 1545 to 1570. The chapel which stands here today was first built in 1884, and is a detailed replica of the original building which had become dilapidated.

The ground makes an ideal spot for drying the egg-sized betel nuts ▶

Church of Our Beloved Lady of the Mountain: In 1510, Alfonso de Albuquerque founded this church, little of which remained similar to the original construction after having been rebuilt three times. The interior houses three altars dedicated to the Saints Mary, Andrew and Anthony.
Monastery and Church of the Miraculous Cross: Only a facade remains of the original home of the miraculous cross which now hangs in the Santa Monica Convent. The Carmelites in the church founded the monastery in 1621. After their extradition in 1707, the buildings began to decay.
From the elevated terrace, which once served as a podium for the altar, is a broad panorama which makes the short walk to the terrace very worthwhile.
Whipping Post: the solitary post on the road to Neura was originally part of a Hindu temple. It later served as a whipping post for the Portuguese colonial authorities. Outlaws like thieves and swindlers were publicly flogged here up until the late 17th century. Heavy iron cuffs, sturdily anchored in the basalt pillar made any attempt to flee impossible. If the infraction was more severe, the convict was then imprisoned in the damp dungeon of Fort Aguada.

Old Goa / **Practical Information**

Travelling to Old Goa: There is a bus service operating regularly from Panjim; the trip lasts half an hour. Most of the buses from Panjim to Ponda also stop in Old Goa.
During certain holidays and festivals, there is ferry service from Panjim. Travel time: 45 minutes.
Accommodation: There is no approved accommodation in Old Goa.

Palolem

Located in the southern province of Canacona and only accessible via a gravel road is the most perfect scenery in Goa: framed by massive boulders, the idyllic bay of Palolem with its beach of fine sand and crystal-clear water remains virtually untouched by tourism. The winged populace from the **Canacona Island** off the coast vie with their human rivals for the best ''nesting" spots.
→*Canacona*

Panjim (Panaji)

Panjim, called ''Panaji" in Hindi and ''Nova Goa" by the colonial rulers has been the capital of Goa, the smallest state in the Indian Union, since 1843.

Panjim, with its picturesque location between the Althinho ridge and the Mandovi River, is home to around 80,000 people, making this Goa's largest city. Panjim does not offer a substantial obligatory programme of sightseeing, but what it does offer is entire older sections of the city dating back to the colonial period which are preserved in their original condition. In addition to this, Panjim can make for a fascinating investigation into Goan daily life, giving the impression that time has come to a standstill. It is nearly impossible to get lost in the city: Panjim was laid out in the chess-board pattern of a Roman "castrum."

Panjim / **History**

Panjim was first mentioned in history almost 900 years ago. An inscription dating back to 1107, during the rule of the Kadambas, mentions a small town called "Pahajuni Kali," "Kali" meaning bay or canal. When the Portuguese arrived, only the small fishing village Taleigao stood where Panjim stands today, protected by the Fort of Adil Khan. A garrison with 300 soldiers enforced customs regulations and patrolled the shipping on the Mandovi from this strategic point, eight kilometres from the Moslem capital, where Old Goa would later be built. On December 15, 1510, revolt broke out against the Portuguese intruders: Antonio de Noronha conquered the fort — and thus became the first Portuguese to be able to sail further up the Mandovi River. In the years to follow, the Portuguese further developed Panjim as a military base, laying out new fortifications. The arriving Governors and viceroys spent their first night in Goa in the former summer residence of Adil Shah. Panjim grew rapidly, especially during the 17th century: "fidalgos," former soldiers who had now advanced to the status of land owners, built their houses here. In 1759, after the terrible epidemic that ravaged Old Goa, Panjim became, for the time being, the residence of the viceroy. In 1843, Panjim went on to become "Nova Goa," the new capital of the Portuguese colony in India, including meanwhile the small northern cities of Daman and Diu as well. Panjim retained the necessary infrastructures from the period from 1827 to 1835. The viceroy Dom Manuel de Portugal e Castro had the slum quarters demolished and had wide representative boulevards, laid out perpendicularly, built in their place. A second building boom came with Goa's independence in 1961. Newly built housing projects provided shelter for the exploding population; the development of education and health care was fostered. Meanwhile, the capital city of Panjim is surrounded by seven military bases and a military airport.

Panjim / **Sights**

The **Hotel Mandovi,** formerly Panjim's premier hotel, makes a good starting point for a stroll through the city. Next door to the hotel is the **Dom Lourenço Chapel** from the 18th century with a collection of coats of arms from the Portuguese emigrants. The **Riverfront Promenade,** called "Campal" by the Goans, has also seen better days. Bordered by a small, tree-lined avenue, it offers some beautiful views of the river, with its constant traffic of barges laden with iron and manganese ore, headed for Mormugao. Formerly, **Fort Aguada,** built in 1612 on the opposite bank, was the customs station for incoming ships. Later, these damp fortification walls served as a prison before the ruins became a popular spot for honeymooners, who flock here by the thousands during December, the month in India for weddings, to renew their vows by sunset. The only link with the north, the Nehru Bridge, collapsed in 1986, shortly after its dedication ceremony in the presence of Premier Rajiv Gandhi.

Past the **Municipal Library,** the small park and three blocks of houses, one will come upon the **Marketplace.** It begins with women sitting on the ground selling fruit from large wicker baskets, wearing saris typical of the region. The lower edge of fabric is wrapped through the legs and tucked into the back of the belt: almost as practical as a pair of trousers.

Depending on the season, eggplant, beans, mangoes, papayas, watermelons, small and very juicy bananas, radishes, garlic and ginger are sometimes available, in addition to the usual wide variety of fruits and vegetables. Even more exotic are the squash-like yak-fruit and breadfruit, which can weigh up to twelve kilograms. In addition, "drumsticks," a fruit with the width of a finger that can grow up to 30 centimetres in length, are prepared as a vegetable and have a flavour similar to asparagus. Among the assortment are also dried or ground dark red chilies, as well as legumes specific to the region and okra, referred to as "lady fingers" by the natives.

Other stands behind those for the fruit and vegetables are clearly organised according to the type of goods sold; fabrics, plastic products, baked goods, spices and much, much more. The coffin maker, the last in the row of stands, signals the end of the marketplace.

After having sufficiently explored and photographed the marketplace, one can then saunter up the Alfonso de Albuquerque Street, the main axial street in Panjim. The building directly to the right is the **Administration Building of Goa, Daman and Diu.** A peek into an open window is always interesting: mounds of files piled everywhere. Quite often, there are five people sitting at one desk, some reading the newspaper, smoking or having a heated discus-

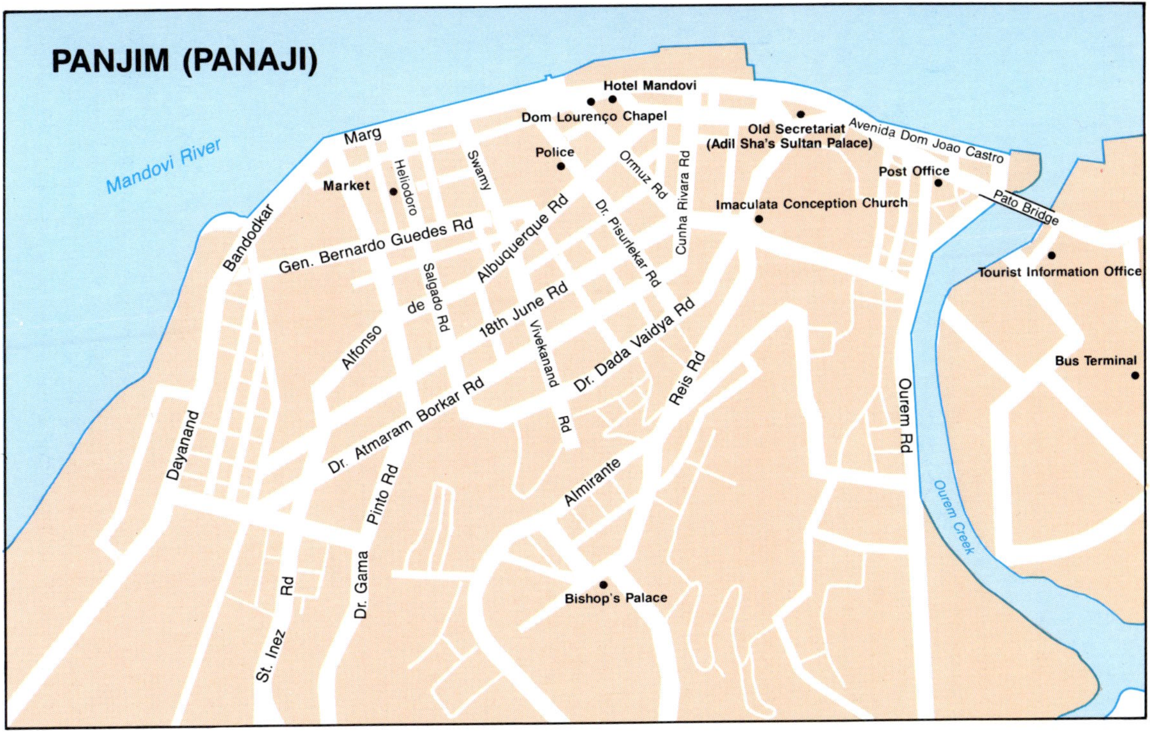
PANJIM (PANAJI)
Mandovi River
Hotel Mandovi
Dom Lourenço Chapel
Old Secretariat
(Adil Sha's Sultan Palace)
Avenida Dom Joao Castro
Post Office
Pato Bridge
Imaculata Conception Church
Tourist Information Office
Bus Terminal
Police
Market
Marg
Heliodoro
Swamy
Ormuz Rd
Cunha Rivara Rd
Dr. Pisurlekar Rd
Albuquerque Rd
Gen. Bernardo Guedes Rd
Bandodkar
Salgado Rd
Alfonso
de
18th June Rd
Vivekanand
Rd
Dr. Dada Vaidya Rd
Reis Rd
Dr. Atmaram Borkar Rd
Pinto Rd
Dr. Gama
St. Inez
Rd
Dayanand
Almirante
Bishop's Palace
Ourem Rd
Ourem Creek

sion. On the ceiling above, the electric fan rotates relentlessly: each pile of papers is weighted down with whatever happened to be handy at the time. Somewhat further along the road, one will come across a tropical green plaza — the **Azad Maidan.** The **Monument of the Unknown Soldier** is guarded day and night, which is of little interest to the youths playing ball on the square. At the end of the oblong church square **Largo da Igreja,** there is an impressive view of the **Church of the Immaculate Conception,** perched above a massive staircase. This church was made Panjim's parish church in 1600. Built in 1540, it ranks among the oldest religious constructions in Goa. A festival is celebrated every year on December 8, in honour of St. Mary, the church's patron saint. The festivities include parades, holy mass and an exuberant folk festival — considered by the residents of Panjim *the* annual event along with the Carnival celebration in February. A religious festival dedicated to Our Lady of Fatima takes place on May 13. The old parish cemetery behind the church had to give way to the ''Corte de Oiteiro" street in 1878. Although Panjim already had some private villas and governors' palaces at the beginning of the 19th century, the area to the front of the church has remained completely untouched by the city's influence. Small fish ponds, rice fields and shabby huts extend to the north ending up at a dingy beach.

Back to the **Harbour.** The ferry which departed from here on the 24-hour journey to Bombay is meanwhile no longer in operation. This harbour is also closed during monsoon season from May to September. Directly adjacent is the first part of the **fishing harbour.** Early risers can experience how the fish are unloaded from the boats and auctioned off immediately in a cacophony of screaming and shouting.

The striking white building with the overhanging roof and wrought-iron balconies in front of the windows is the old **Sultan's Palace of Adil Shah,** also called **The Old Secretariat.** This was the former residence of the viceroys and governor generals of Goa. From here, they ruled the colony from the year 1759. Today, this impressive building serves as accommodation for the Lieutenant General's guests of state. The palace was built in 1594 to serve a completely different purpose: the Franciscan monks used it as a cloister.

Continuing straight ahead, one will pass by the ''GPO," the main post office. Behind the post office is the beginning of the city's districts called **San Tomé,** formerly called ''Largo da Estanco," and **Fontainhas,** which are still quite reminiscent of the earlier colonial period: narrow alleyways run through both of these districts, one also finds lattice balconies, wooden shutters which close from the inside, colourful Azuelejos tiles, potted plants in full bloom and roaming cats — impressions like those from the Portuguese homeland. Earlier, the "fidalgos," soldiers who had become landowners, settled here. This earlier development remains evident on many of the nameplates today: names like Menezes, Cavalho, Almeido and Rodrigues can be seen on many of the doors. Melancholy music can be heard from the small pubs and liquor shops. The residents often reach for the guitar; lost in contemplation, they pluck out almost forgotten melodies and sing their fados in a scruffy voice, musically escaping the present.

A nice conclusion to a sight-seeing tour through Panjim is a stroll through the **Althinho,** the residential area preferred by the nouveau riche of Panjim. The **Patriarchal Palace** stands at the highest point, surrounded by villas belonging to the local prominence. It is the view, however, which makes the walk most worthwhile: an impressive panorama of the city on the banks of the Mandovi River.

Panjim / **Practical Information**

Accommodation: *I. Western Style*

Hotel Mandovi, Bandodkar Marg, Tel: 22 85 (five telephone lines), Telex: 0194-226.

Hotel Vistar, Rua Alfonso de Albuquerque, Tel: 35 82 or 21 94.

Hotel Soan, Rua de Querem, Tel: 33 04.

Hotel Aroma, Gunha Rivara Road (across from the city park), Tel: 35 19.

Flaming Hotel, Rua de Querem, Tel: 27 65.

Tourist Hotel, Tel: 23 03.

Giumaka Guest House, Wolfango de Silva Road (near Cine Samrat-Ashok).

Hotel Samrat, Dada Vaidya Road, Tel: 33 39.

II. Indian Style

In Goa "Indian Style" means more simple, less expensive, less tidy, but also often more centrally located. Most of these less expensive quarters are located in the older areas of the city around the General Post Office.

Central Lodge P.O., Tel: 29 92.

Church Side Lodge (near the Parish Church of the Immaculate Conception).

Corina Lodge, next to the General Post Office.

Danuz Hotel, Luis de Menezes Road.

Glemar Lodge, next to the nature park.

Goa Lodge, Alfonso de Albuquerque Road, Tel: 25 52.

Hotel Imperial, next to the bus station.

Hotel Central, Campel.

Riviera, Rua de Ormuz, Tel: 24 18.

Hotel Madhavashram, near the Hotel Mandovi, Tel: 28 23.
Hotel Sangam, Mala, Tel: 23 07.
Hotel Venite, 31st January Road.
Indian Niwas, near the Cine El Dorado, Tel: 27 59.
Kismet Lodge, near the municipal market.
Lavista Lodge, near the Pato Bridge, Rua de Querem, Tel: 27 65.
Liberty Guest House, near the Don Bosco High School, Tel: 32 19.
Palace Hotel, behind the Secretary Building, Tel: 28 10.
Safari Hotel, across from the city park.
Samman Lodge, 18th June Road, Tel: 35 17.
Shree Rameshwar Hindu Lodging, near the Mahalaxmi Temples, Tel: 27 76.
Sunder Lodge, Canetano de Albuquerques Road, Tel: 33 26.
Temperine Guest House, Rua Alfonso de Albuquerque.
Kohinoor Lodge, near the Cine Samrat-Ashok.
La Vista Lodge, near the General Post Office.
Hotel Republica Lodging, across from the Secretary Building, Tel: 26 30.

The square in front of the Holy Ghost Church in Margao is surrounded by 300-year-old colonial villas

The **Youth Hostel** can be reached via the road along the shore called Dayanand Bandodkar Marg. The hostel is located in a side street shortly after the municipal sport complex, only minutes from Miramar Beach. Tel: 54 33.

Automobile Club: W.I.A.A., Tourist Hotel.

Automobile Repairs: Angle's Auto Centre, Dr. Shigaonkar Road, Tel: 43 81; B.N. Thakur Garage (Fiat), Tel: 32 52/32 51; Mandovi-Motors (Volkswagen), Tonca, Tel: 31 07; Garage Matmo, Dada Vaidya Road, Tel: 31 13.

Book Store: Hotel Mandovi, Hotel Fidalgo.

Bus Companies: Karnataka State Road Transport corporation (KSRTC), Bus Terminus, Tel: 51 26; Maharashtra SRTC, Bus Complex, Tel: 43 63; Maharashtra Tourism Development Corporation (MTDC), Tourist Hostel, Tel: 35 72; Kadamba Transport Corporation, Bus Terminus, Tel: 33 34; West Coast Travels, Old Bus Stand, Tel: 57 23.

Car Rentals: GTDC, Tourist Home, Tel: 33 96 or 39 03.

Foreign Registration Office: Police Headquarters (for those staying for a longer period).

The Aga Khan Park in Margao is a paradise for children

Hospital: Tel: 45 66 (Ambulance: Tel: 30 26).
Lawyer: Vasco da Silva Ferreira.
Pharmacies: Cosme Matias Menezes, 31 Janetro Road, Tel: 29 65; Menezes & Cia., near the General Post Office, Tel: 29 17 ; Farmacia Salcete, across from the Public Health Department, Tel: 33 50; Hindu Pharmacy, across from the Municipal Gardens, Tel: 25 76.
Physician: Dr. Irene A. Barreto-Menezes, Rua de Quercem, Tel: 58 40.
Police: Dr. Pisurlenkar Road/corner of Alfonso de Albuquerque Road, Tel: 1 00.
Post Office and Telephones: General Post Office (GPO), Tel: 37 04, counter for general delivery letters (poste restante).
Restaurants: Restaurant in the Hotel Mandovi: second floor, international and regional cuisine from excellent to horrible, slow service, but with a balcony overlooking the Mandovi River.
Chit-Chat Restaurant: in the Tourist Hotel, second floor, lovely veranda, closed Saturdays, Tel: 23 03.
Restaurant in the Hotel Venite: behind the post office, very cozy ambiance in an old house with wooden floors and original Portuguese cuisine.
New Punjab Restaurant: near the city park, good tandoori dishes, somewhat more expensive.
El Gazella: Campal, Tel: 20 19.
Shalimar Restaurant: across from the Government Printing Press, Tel: 23 36.
Taj Mahal: vegetarian restaurant, across from the Government Printing Press, Alfonso de Albuquerque road, Tel: 24 46.
La Alegro Restaurant: Santa Inez, Shanta Building.
Olympic Restaurant: across from the Customs Building.
Sher-e-Punjab Restaurant & Chinese Restaurant: near the Health Office, Tel: 20 65.
Riverside: across from the Hotel Mandovi with a dining terrace on the banks of the Mandovi River, very good pomfret dishes.
Shanbhag: vegetarian restaurant, across from the city park.
Goenchin: Dr. Dada Vaidya Road, Chinese cuisine, very good and quite expensive.
Bakeries: in the Hotel Mandovi (next to the book store); A Pasteria, next to Goenchin, Dr. Dada Vaidya Road.
Sports: Panjim Gymkhana (fitness centre), Campal, Tel: 58 18; Tennis: club complex on Gaspar-Diaz-Beach, Tel: 38 62.
Taxation Office: Shanta Building, 18th June Road. Important when leaving the country after a visit lasting more than 90 days.

Tourist Information: Department of Tourism, Rua Alfonso de Albuquerque, Tel: 26 73. The neighbouring states also have public Tourist Information Offices in Panjim: Maharashtra Tourist Information Bureau, Tourist Hostel, Tel: 35 72; Karnataka Tourist Information Centre, Boca de Vaca, Tel: 20 46; Andhra Pradesh Tourist Information Centre, Rua de Querem.

Train Tickets: Reservations are taken under the telephone number 56 20 from 9:30 am to 1 pm/2:30 to 5 pm.

Transportation: Travelling south, buses depart from the central bus station. The trip to Vasco and Mormugao lasts a little over an hour. There are two routes to Margao: the shorter route via Agassim and Cortalim takes an hour and a half; the longer of the two routes via Ponda takes almost two and a half hours. There is city bus service departing regularly for Old Goa. Travelling north, buses depart from Betim on the north bank of the Mandovi. Old ferries continually bring the masses of people to Betim. Buses to Calangute operate until late into the evening. The somewhat longer route via Saligao is worth taking because of the unparalleled view of the pastoral landscape of rolling hills to the north. Mapusa is only 30 minutes away from Panjim, taking the N 17 motorway; this monotone stretch of motorway provides little diversion.

Travel Agencies: Georgeson, across from the main post office, Tel: 21 50, also has a branch in Calangute; Tradewings, 6 Mascarenhas Building, Alfonso de Albuquerque Road, Tel: 42 35, 51 78, 49 30; Mandovi Tours & Travels, near the main post office, Tel: 59 62.

Panjim / **Surroundings**

Dayanand Bandodkar Marg District: In the lowlands of Campal, where expanses of swampland where rice fields and palm groves once were, is now Panjim's representative district. It was named after Goa's first Chief Minister after Goa became independent. In addition to the modern housing complexes for the middle class of Panjim, the "Menezes Bragança Institute," the Goan Academy of Fine Arts, is also located here.

Ourem Creek: Numerous small salt ponds characterise the landscape of the small bay in the eastern portion of Panjim.

Reis Magos Church: This church is located on the northern bank toward Aguada, seven kilometres from Panjim. Built in 1555, it was the first church in the Bardez Province, and one of the first churches in Goa. The impressive church is dedicated to the three wise men from the Orient, Kaspar, Melchior and Belshazzar. Inside the church, once a Franciscan mission, the future viceroys were confirmed into office on the day after their arrival from Portugal during a ceremonial mass.

The floor, covered with inscriptions, is very interesting. The inlaid grave slabs reveal that seven Portuguese viceroys and governors were buried here. An underground tunnel, the entrance of which is cleverly hidden behind the stairway, connected the church to the nearby fort.

Every year, on January 6, newlywed couples organise the "Reis Magos Festival." This is the climax of the "Fair dos Reis" (5-7 January), a big folk festival which was celebrated earlier within the protection of the fort's walls in the presence of the viceroy and the archbishop.

Reis Magos Fort: The fort was built in 1551, under the rule of the viceroy Dom Alfonso de Noronha on the ruins of a small fort built by Adil Shah. Dom Francisco da Gama had the fort expanded before it was replaced completely by a more modern construction by Viceroy Caetano da Melo e Castro in 1704. Underneath the fortress, seven casemates lead almost forty meters into the laterite stone. However, the fort served not only military functions. In the past century, as reported by the *Gazetteer of Goa,* Madhav Rao, the Raja of Sawantwadi slept here during a state visit, along with his 1500 men, 1000 horses and four elephants.

Colegio Real: The two-story collegium, which, like the church, was founded in 1555, served as an administrative seat for numerous viceroys from 1597 to 1793.

Paroda

Paroda is a village with 2,000 residents, located 11 kilometres south of Margao. Worth seeing is the **Shri Chandranath Temple.** Located on the summit of the 350 metre high Chandranath, this temple built from black basalt offers a fabulous view. Shiva is worshipped here as "Chandranatha," the Lord of the Moon. The statue of the Shivalingam is said to have supernatural properties: if the moonlight shines on the stone, water drops seep out of the Lingam. For those who don't believe this: go to the temple during full moon — only then does moonlight shine onto the stone.

Despite the signs of deterioration, this villa on the old marketplace in Margao still reflects its former grandeur ▶

Fantasia
Arts Corner

Partagal

Partagal is a small town in the southern province of Canacona on the northern bank of the Talpona. The religious centres of the "madhavas" or "vishnavas," the Brahman followers belonging to the Vishnu cult, can be found here.

People

In 1981, 1,007,749 Goans were registered in the census which takes place every ten years — of these, about half are of the Catholic faith and a third are Hindus or Moslems. Hindi, English, Portuguese, Konkani and Marathi (the official language in the neighbouring state of Maharashtra) are considered languages of equal status in Goa, a state with an area of 3,702 square kilometres. Measured by Indian standards, the Goans are doing quite well financially. With the exception of Delhi, Goans have the highest annual income, averaging 3,500 Rupees per person. The overall average in India is 2,500 Rupees. As a comparison: a street worker, who carries the stones from the street in round brass bowls, is paid about two Rupees per day. In addition to the good agricultural base and infrastructure from colonial times, Goa's "wealth" is especially a result of the growing tourism and also stems from the money sent from the Gulf States, where at least one member of every household is employed.
In Pompurpa, a small village north of the Mandovi, the women, whose husbands are working far away from home in Arabia, leave their husbands' shoes in front of the door. Upon their return, it would then seem like they had just come back from a day's work in the fields. Goa's population is presently in a state of upheaval: while more and more Goans go to the Gulf States to find work, more and more "foreigners" move to Goa in search of work. The newcomers, usually Hindus from other parts of India, already make up a third of the population. Their clay huts which sprout up around the factories present a predicament for Goa — and a shock for the tourists who arrive at Dabolim: they are usually appalled at the slums surrounding the Birli chemical plant not far from the airport.

During elections, Christians and Hindus are regularly pitted against each other. The immigration of Hindus from the poorer states bordering Goa is not officially sanctioned by Delhi, but the central government is not unhappy to see this development. The Goans view this matter differently. Slogans like "Goa for the Goans" are painted on buildings at night in bright red letters — and just as regularly, washed back off by the monsoon rains.

Even before this foreign infiltration, Goa had developed a strange mixture of the two value systems over the centuries due to the close coexistence of Christians and Hindus. The Christian attribute of human equality also failed in Goa in light of Indian reality. It did, however, weaken the Hindu caste system. Christians in Goa have also firmly integrated the Indian pantheon based on Vishnu and Shiva into their own religious beliefs.

Not only the Hindu temples are based on architectural fragments imported from the Catholic Church — whether the dark blue Azuelejos tiles or the brass incense burners — but the key positions in industry, politics and culture are now as ever occupied by Christians. The Hindus rank among the poorer social strata. As is the case with the Moslems who have sought seclusion in the area around Ponda where their main mosque is located, the Hindus also live geographically isolated from the Catholics. Their houses can be easily recognised: a brightly painted "Tulsi" stands in front of the door dedicated to a popular deity. Planted near the statue's pedestal, which includes the characteristic symbols of the god, is a basil tree. If watered daily, the god is appeased and ensures happiness and prosperity for the residents.

Pernem

About 6,000 residents live in Pernem, the capital of the northernmost province of Goa, located 28 kilometres north of Panjim and 14 kilometres north of Mapusa.

Here, the **Shri Bhagvati Temple** is worth seeing. The temple, directly on the thoroughfare N 17, is presumed to be over 500 years old. Two life-size statues of elephants, made from black stone, guard the entrance. Perched on a high pedestal is an almost two metre high statue of the goddess Bahagwati-Astabhuja. During the Dussehra Festival, celebrated for ten days in October, more than 25,000 devout Hindus make Paroda the goal of their pilgrimage each year.

Photography

Be sure to bring enough film with you. If you find yourself running short on film, colour film (usually Kodak) is available in Goa. However the film does not keep well in the heat and the expiration dates are often exceeded. After exposing a roll of film, be sure to put it back in the film container and store it in a cool place — the mini-bar in the hotel room is a good place. This is

the only way to ensure that the colour quality will survive the temperatures. Even when staying for a longer period of time, one should not have film developed in Goa because the chemicals are often obsolete or have turned. In general, photos may be taken everywhere; only the airports, train stations, bridgeheads as well as all governmental ministries, councils and courts are exceptions to this rule. Therefore, tourists may not photograph the picturesque and impressive Governor's Palace — the police become quite apparent if one wishes to photograph it. Children, on the other hand, love to have their picture taken. If, however, someone turns away or shakes his head rejectingly, this should be respected — Goa and its residents are not an exotic outdoor museum.
Sometimes a modest Bakshish (tip) helps. A camera fee often must be paid for video taping; in some places, filming is even strictly forbidden.

Pilar

Pilar is located 11 kilometres south of Panjim. The former capital of the Kadamba queen lay on the fertile peninsula of Tissuari, on which predominantly vegetable crops are grown. On the site where the Kadamba mansion displayed its radiance and splendour in the 7th and 8th centuries, today there is only a signpost in among the palm trees which reads: For the Portuguese conquerors, this was the location of "Goa Velha," Old Goa.
Pilar Monastery: Located two kilometres to the north, the monastery is accessible by way of a small country road which branches off directly after the palm grove. Franciscan monks founded this complex on July 17, 1613. In 1633, a "University of Sciences, Fine Arts and Theology" was added. When the order was banned on May 28, 1834, the monastery became the property of the state. Since then, it has continued to slowly deteriorate. The courtyard may be visited. There, there is an altar with posts ornamented with intricately carved figures. The church, which has several wooden alters covered with gold leaf, also has a remarkable pulpit. Frater Agnelo's grave is a popular goal of pilgrimages for Goan Catholics.
The location of the monastery is ideal: the view extends from far beyond the Zuari River all the way to the harbour of Mormugao.

The colourful activity makes the marketplace in Margao definitely worth visiting ▶

Ponda

Ponda, the gateway to the Westghats, is located about 30 kilometres from Panjim on the A4. the small industrial city has remained the centre of the goan mining industry. On the surrounding slopes, manganese, magnesium, iron ore and bauxite silicates are mined.

Ponda / **History**

Up until 1763, this city was a Hindu enclave of the Mahratta princes. It was only 250 years after Goa was conquered that Ponda was incorporated into the Portuguese colony. Even today, Ponda remains a religious centre for Goan Hinduism. The Hindu's religious tolerance prompted Moslems to settle here as well.

Ponda / **Sights**

Safa Shahouri Masjid Mosque: Of the 27 Mosques that formerly stood around Ponda, only one remains: the Safa Shahouri Masjid Mosque. It was built in 1560 by Ibrahim Adil Shah of Bijapur. Before being repeatedly destroyed by the Portuguese, the mosque was surrounded by extensive gardens with a number of fountains. The two surpreme Islamic holidays, Id Ul-Fitr and Id Ud-Duha, are celebrated here every year with tremendous pomp.

Postal System

In India, there is a high level of inflation which pushes up the postal rates. In 1990 the rate for a postcard was 4 Rs.; for letters (20 g) 6.50 Rs. ''air mail" must appear on the letter to ensure a more speedy delivery. Important letters should be brought directly to the post office — many a letter has become lost at the hotel reception. Eight to ten days are required for a letter to reach Europe. General delivery letters are collected at the General Post Office (GPO) in the centre of Panjim.

Poverim

The small town of Poverim on the national road from Panjim to Mapusa is famous among visitors to northern Goa: this is where the restaurant ''O Coqueiro" offers ''homesick service" with the quickest telephone connections from Goa to home.

In the Xavier Centre for Historical Research, Tel: 46 97, both secular and theological scientists are dedicated to researching the religious and social history of Goa.

Poverim / **Restaurants**

O Coqueiro: Spacious restaurant with a terrace, a large garden and a hint of Portuguese flair.
The extensive menu offers excellent seafood, curries and tandoori dishes — fiery, fruity, formidable. Because occasional live concerts take place here, reservations are recommended. Tel: 25 71. The restaurant destined to play a role in an infamous incident: the internationally sought after mass murderer Charles Sobhraj was arrested here after his daring escape from prison in New Delhi.

Press

India's larger national newspapers, including some articles on foreign affairs and international news are: *The Times of India, Hindustan Times, Indian Express,* and *The Statesman.* The local paper *The Navhind Times* provides interesting coverage of local news. This newspaper is not only an informative reflection of the society, but was also the theme of a song sung by the pop star Remo, which included a portion of fondness as well as irony.

Press / **History**

In 1821, the *Gazzeta de Goa,* the first newspaper for India as a whole, was printed in Goa. The Government Printing Press set up their heavy machinery for lead typesetting in Adil Shah's former sultan's palace. In 1837, the first official gazette *Boletim do Governo do Estado da India* appeared twice a week until it was integrated into the *Official Gazette of the Government of Goa* in 1961. *O Heraldo,* the first Portuguese daily newspaper, appeared on January 22, 1900. This paper, founded by Professor Messias Gomes, went out of production on October 10, 1983. The first Portuguese tabloid, called *Diario da Noite,* appeared on December 1, 1919. Luis de Menezes, the founder, already had the first issue printed fully automatically and in colour. Only thirty years later did this modern technology reach the country of Portugal. The first weekly newspaper in the English language, *The Times of Goa,* was founded in 1885. In 1963, the first daily Goan newspaper in English appeared, *The Navhind Times.*

Priol

Located 22 kilometres from Panjim on the national thoroughfare to Ponda, this small town serves as a starting point for a tour to the most significant Hindu temple in Goa.

Priol / **Sights**

Shri Mangueshi Temple: The over 400-year-old Shri Mangueshi Temple is considered to be Goa's most beautiful Hindu temple. As was the case with most of the other temples, it was moved to this location from the coast after the Portuguese conquest. In this temple, Hindus venerated Shiva as "Manguesha," Lord of the Mountains. An old legend explains this name: Shiva and Parvati, his spouse, often passed the time by playing dice. When Parvati lost one day, she left Shiva in a rage. Her wanderings led her to Goa where she came across a huge tiger. In her panic, she yelled for help: "Tvahi Manis Girish — Lord of the Mountains, save me!" Shiva came immediately to her

With an appearance more similar to a lake, the Mandovi River near Panjim

rescue and saved his spouse from the jaws of the tiger, leaving behind, as a sign, the symbol of his power, the lingam.

At the front of the parking area, a short processional path leads by peddlers selling coconuts and kitsch to the holy pond, where even today, Hindu women still wash their laundry in the cloudy water. Traditional cleansings and ritual water offerings, however, no longer take place here. On the steps up to the temple gates, farmers' wives and children sell colourful flower garlands and lotus blossoms, which are later placed in the offering plate along with pieces of coconut and money. Through the gate, one enters a courtyard bordered on three sides by pilgrim quarters. A radiant white dipmal, a lamppost in the form of steps, so typical for Goa, is decorated at its base with the emblems of Shiva, Brahma and Ganesha. The swastika is a widespread symbol of fertility in India. Its origin dates back to the Aryan immigration to the Indus valley around 3000 B.C.

Before entering the central temple hall, one must remove one's shoes. For a few Rupees, temple servants will also protect them from the pilfering apes.

The brilliant white of the parish church in Panjim against the background of the deep blue sky

The threshold between the foyer, the "mandapa," and the inner sanctuary should not be crossed first by the left foot. Otherwise, folklore warns, one is in danger of tragedy and misfortune.
The columns, painted blue, the colour of Shiva, depict the deity as "Nataraj," a dancing god, who destroys the evil in the world with a wreath of fire to make room for the good, the new, and life's creative powers. Crystal chandeliers can be found all over Goa: they were brought from Venice and were very popular during the 18th and 19th centuries.

Prohibition

In contrast to the other states in the Indian Union, there is no prohibition in Goa. The result of this is obvious, especially with the Indians from the neighbouring states, where a strict ban on alcohol is enforced: during the weekends, Goa becomes a Mecca for the ardent imbibers, who can be found in doorways, on park benches or lying on the sidewalks during the evening, worn out from the exhausting day of drinking, and sleeping off their alcohol-induced euphoria.
Locally produced alcoholic beverages are extremely inexpensive in Goa; on the other hand foreign brands demand horrendous prices. If a local product or "Indian made foreign liquors" (IMFL) are not explicitly ordered, the waiter will always serve expensive imported brands.

Railways →*Transportation*

Religion

Catholicism was the official religion in Goa, which meant a high degree of oppression for the Hindu and Moslem minorities over the centuries, including the intentional attempt to eradicate these minorities altogether. Today, 35% of the Goanese refer to themselves as Catholics. 60% of the population are Hindu and three percent worship Allah and follow the teachings of the Koran. The remaining two percent of Goa's population are Jains, Sikhs or Parsen, all members of the religious community founded by Zarathustra.
The most popular deities among the Hindus are Shiva, Vishnu, Ganesha and Durga. The farmers and simple labourers have taken an especial liking to Krishna. Because it is left up to each person, how many gods he worships

(if any at all), there is always a confusing multitude of deities being honoured. Many paths of experiencing the god are open to the Hindus: gods can be honoured through trees, animals, a fetish or merely in spirit. Coming closer to the gods can be accomplished through frenzied dances, brutal blood offerings, asceticism, meditation or a pilgrimage. After all, every god also has different ''aspects,'' meaning manifestations, in which he reveals himself. Therefore, it is often difficult for outsiders, who have not grown up within this religion to relate to the pictures in the temples and the symbols of a specific deity. Still, there are distinguishing characteristics, that apply to the individual gods specifically.

Brahma: Once venerated as the highest deity of the world, the ''creator of the world'' is more likely unpopular with the masses today. The typical portrayal of Brahma is with four arms and a head that looks into all four directions simultaneously. In his four hands, he holds the insignia of his power: a spoon for cleansing ceremonies, a wreath of roses, the old Vedic scriptures, and a bowl containing holy water.

Shiva: Shiva, also called ''Mahadeva'' (the great god), ranks among the most popular gods in Goa. This deity, the husband of Parvati and the father of Ganesha, is venerated as the concept of life. He embodies the destructive and creative powers of life, as shown by his two faces. Popular portrayals of Shiva are as ''Nataraj,'' dancing on the globe in the middle of a wreath of fire. his symbol, the lingam, an erect phallus, is not missing in any temple. In his four hands, Shiva carries the symbols of his power: a trident, an antelope, a lasso to capture his enemies and a musical instrument similar to a drum. Shiva's spouse is appropriately as many-sided as Shiva himself.

Durga (Kali/Parvati/Shakti/Uma): Shiva and his wife Parvati, the daughter of the mountain king Himalaya, is the only divine duo in the Indian Pantheon that share equal power. As Durga, Shiva's wife fights and conquers demons that threaten mankind. In contrast, as Kali, she transfigures herself into a blood-hungry beast, which can only be appeased with blood offerings. As the incarnation of the unshackled energy of life, she is called Shakti; as the merciful and forgiving mother of mankind, she is worshipped as Uma. Shiva's spouse is often depicted accompanied by a lion.

Ganesha: An old legend in the Ramayana tells of the fate of Ganesha, the son of Shiva and Parvati, who has the head of an elephant. Upon returning to his wife Parvati after a journey lasting several years, Shiva found the bedroom door locked. Inside, he heard the voices of his wife and another man. Overcome with rage, he broke the lock and jumped onto the bed and cut off the head of the presumed lover. In tears, Parvati told Shiva that he had killed his own son. To save his son, Shiva sacrificed his most loyal companion and placed the head onto the body of his son — the head was that of an elephant. The Goanese worship Ganesha as the god of wisdom, learning and success. If they open up a shop, take their exams or publish a book, a ceremony is held beforehand to venerate Ganesha. Ganesha's characteristic attributes are, in addition to the hatchet, a cane and a prayer wreath. He travels on the back of a rat.

Nandir: The steer ridden by Shiva.

Vishnu: Vishnu, preserver of the world, appears when mankind is in danger. He has appeared on the earth nine times, each time as a different incarnation. In his most recent incarnation, he took on the form of Buddha. The Hindus expect his tenth incarnation, as ''Kalki,'' in the near future. Vishnu possesses animal and human aspects. His bodily incarnations (atavaras) are: fish, turtle, boar, lion, dwarf, Parasurama, Rama, Krishna and Buddha. His characteristic symbol is a discus with a sharp edge, with which he can behead his enemies. Occasionally, he also carries a club or a large stone in his hand. The gentler side of Vishnu's character is symbolized by the lotus blossom, sometimes also a seashell. Vishnu rides on the back of the sacred bird Garuda.

Lakshmi: Vishnu's subordinate spouse, often worshipped as the goddess of beauty, love and happiness. She is often depicted sitting in a lotus blossom, while elephants spout water onto her hair.

Krishna: The divine prankster is often portrayed in blue. The god of the shepherds, who supposedly loved more than 450 women during his youth, enjoys passing the time by playing the flute. Sometimes he stands on a snake, his left hand around its body and holding a lotus blossom in his right hand.

→*Holidays and Celebrations*

Saligao

Saligao is 13 kilometres north of Panjim, located in the direction of Calangute. The highest point on the series of hills offers a majestic panorama.

Saligao / **Sights**

Mae de Deus (Mother of God) Church: The church was built in 1873 in Neo-Gothic architecture. The Mother of God Shrine was transported here from the ruins of the Mae de Deus Convent in Old Goa.

Mother of God Seminary: Around 110 priests receive their first instruction in the priesthood before visiting the Rachol Seminary near Raia for further education.

Sanguem

The capital city of the Sanguem province lies 25 kilometres southeast of Margao on the Zuari River.
The Mosque Jama Masjid, built in the 19th century and restored in the mid 1950's, is worth seeing.

Sanquelim

Sanquelim is located 37 kilometres from Panjim. A population of approximately 4000 is dispersed among 10 townships.
Shri Datta Mandir: Used as a sanatorium for men with "impure thoughts," this Trimurthi temple is known throughout the entire country. In December, the famous Datta Jayanti Festival takes place, attracting the faithful from the neighbouring Indian states. The 100-year-old temple is surrounded by slender betel palm trees.

Not limousines, but motor scooters are parked in front of the Governor's Palace in Panjim

Sanvordem

Sanvordem is a small village with a train station located on the Zuari River. The **country residence of the Mirandra family** is located here. The Mirandra family will receive interested parties who have arranged a visit in advance in their over 300-year-old colonial villa. The interior has hardly been changed since the villa's construction. At most, it has been only supplemented by a few modern objects. In the Banquet Hall on the second floor, the son who lives in Delhi has set up a private sales exhibition. His modern paintings are in high demand among Indian art collectors.

The shady inner courtyard is a small, tropical idyll: aromatic frangipani trees, bright violet cascades of bougainvillea, some poinsettias and countless terra cotta flower urns filled with flowers and cuttings make for an unparalleled atmosphere.

Shopping

There are no regular business hours in Goa. Generally, the stores are open from 9:30 am to 12:30 pm and then are reopened from 3 to 7 pm. The hotel shops with handmade artifacts, rugs, clothing, jewellry and books have adapted to the daily routine set by the tourists — they open and close later in the day. Popular souvenirs from Goa are the inexpensive cashews. Plain, salted or seasoned with various spices, a kilogramme costs about £ 4 ($6.85). In contrast, a bottle of Feni cashew liqueur is higher in price as well as alcohol content. Also inexpensive are the spices and authentic saffron. If a visitor decides to take home the generic spice ''curry,“ he will find himself confronted by a vast selection: for every dish there is a special masala spice mixture. Sniff out the mixture best suited to your taste. The small packets cost only pennies. Textiles available are cotton, seersucker and pure silks — but one should be cautious: artificial silk is also in fashion in India. Use the burn test on a sample of the material: if the fabric instantly melts into a unsightly clump, the ''genuine“ silk was not worth the price paid.

The markets are nothing short of ideal for shopping:

Panjim: daily

Vasco: daily, good spices, few articles of clothing

Mapusa: Fridays, famous for its clothing

Margao: daily, spread over a number of streets and bazaars, lunch break!

Anjuna: Wednesdays 2 to 7 pm, Indian souvenirs, groceries, clothing, jewellry.

Quepem: Sundays, weekly market

A short trip to the state-run retail outlets of "Goa Handicrafts" is also worthwhile. Since 1966, these stores located throughout India and offering a selection of regional products support the traditional home production of the villages and small local industries. Included in the selection of handcrafted products that are sold in these stores at set prices are: brass wares from Bicholim, lacquered and lathed work from Cuncolim as well as patchwork bags and other textile products. Other states in the Indian Union are also represented in Goa by their official outlet stores.

* Goa Handicrafts, Rural and Small Scale Industries Development, Emporia Shop, Tourist Hotel, Panjim, Mapusa and Vasco

* Kashmir Government Arts Emporium / Kerala Art Crafts, Hotel Fidalgo, Swami Vivekananda Road, Panjim

Sirigal (Sirigao)

Five kilometres from Sanguem is the small village of Sirigal, which is trying to attract more tourism as a supplemental source of income through an ambitious irrigation project. The Salauli Project would produce an artificial lake. Presently the construction of an earthen dam is under way. Measuring 1.3 kilometres in length and almost 43 metres high, this dam will transform the upper course of the Zuari River (called Salauli locally) into a reservoir with an area of 24 square kilometres. Nine villages are already under water as a result of this project. According to the Goan government's Department of Tourism, this reservoir will be approved for water sports and fishing. Beaches for swimming, picnic areas, several hiking paths and simply furnished tourist cottages to house future guests are also in the planning stage. The opening ceremonies are planned during 1991. However, until the Salauli project is completed another event serves as the attraction in this region: on religious holidays, members of the Shiva cult walk over beds of hot coals.

Spices

Spices are the soul of Indian cuisine. In Goa as well, at least half of the long list of ingredients in any cookbook is taken up by spices. Belonging to an Indian chef's essential repertoire are always cardamom, cloves, caraway seed, garlic, ginger, pepper, mustard seed, saffron and cinnamon; either whole or ground into a fine powder. The first conquerors seem to have found these yet unknown spices pleasing to the palate — they brought them back to Europe, revolutionising not only the Christian paradigm but the European cooking as well. Pepper, cloves and cinnamon, which at that time sold at exorbitant prices, began their successful crusade throughout European kitchens. Contrary to the European habits of that time, the Indians never used spices singly, but mixed. Theses ''masalas" are mixed differently according to region, indigenous custom or religious motive. The proportions of the individual spices give each individual dish its own characteristic flavour. For Europeans, the ''Madras-Masala" is highly akin to fire. The generic spice called ''curry" evolved from ''Garam Masala," a mixture of cinnamon, cardamom, cloves, coriander, caraway and pepper. Goans are partial to ''Garam Masala" when seasoning vegetarian dishes, ''Xacuti Masala," on the other hand, is used in a vegetable oil sauce to season all hot meat dishes whether shrimp, beef, lamb or pork. In India the word ''curry" is used as a designation for complete main dishes comprised of either beef, vegetables or fish. Dry curries are called ''baffat" in India. A particular delicacy: pork baffat — shortly before the aromatic sauce is ready to serve, slices of the mild Indian radish are added.

→*Cuisine*

Sports

Cycling: Bicycle rentals can be found in the south of Goa at Hotel Majorda Beach, and in the north they can be rented from the numerous peddlers.

Fitness: Gyms with body-building equipment can be found in the hotels Oberoi Bogmalo, Majorda Beach and Cidade de Goa (all equipped with saunas).

Hiking: Guided hikes are organised by The Hiking Association of Goa, Daman & Diu, c/o Captain A. Rebello (President), Captain of the Ports Office, Panjim, Tel: 50 70. Some marked hiking paths begin at Molem National Park: Tambdi Surla (12 km), Dudhsagar Waterfalls (16 km), Mahavir Wildpark / Atolle Gad (10 km), Matkonda Mountain (2000 ft, 680 m; 10 km).

Parachute Sailing: Oberoi Bogmalo

Sailing: Sail boats are available through the hotels Cidade de Goa, Fort Aguada and The Leela Beach. Further information is available through: Yachting Association, P.O. Box 33, Panjim, Tel: 32 61.

Table Tennis: Tables and equipment rentals are available at the hotels Fort Aguada, Oberoi Bogmalo and Cidade de Goa.

Tennis: Tennis courts are available at the hotels Oberoi Bogmalo, Majorda Beach, Fort Aguada, Cidade de Goa and The Leela Beach.

Water Sports: Information on all types of water sports is available from Aqua Sport, 2nd Floor, Ghanekar Building, Jose Falcao Road, Panjim, Tel: 47 06.
Water Skiing: Lessons and rentals are available in the hotels Fort Aguada, Oberoi Bogmalo, Majorda Beach, Cidade de Goa and The Leela Beach.
Wind Surfing: Lessons and surfboard rentals are available in the hotels Fort Aguada, Oberoi Bogmalo, Majorda Beach, Cidade de Goa and The Leela Beach.

State and Government

Goa, the 23rd state in the Indian Union, is governed by a parliamentary democracy. Up until 1987, Goa was considered a territory under the direct control of Delhi. The Chief Governor was supported by the Chief Minister and the Council of Ministers. Together, they formed the Legislative Assembly of 30 representatives, elected to office for a five-year term. The Legislative Assembly, in turn, sent two representatives to the Raiya Sabha (upper house), representing the individual states in Delhi. After Goa was declared a state in the Indian union, very little changed in the political structures. The most important difference was that the Goan Christians were no longer helplessly subject to the Hindu government in the north, but were given their own legislative assembly. Of the 33 members, 30 are elected by secret ballot; only three are appointed by the head of state, the governor. Now, two elected and one appointed congressmen represent the interests of Goa in New Delhi. The Goan government is, however, still subject to the good will of the federal government in Delhi: both the premier and the president can dissolve the Goan government against their will.
On the local level of government, the ''Panchayat,'' the council of five elders, assumes the responsibility of municipal administration and jurisdiction responsibilities. 194 such local administrative bodies were registered in the census in 1981. The federal responsibilities in Delhi include defence, foreign policy, currency and credit, transportation, customs and taxes. Goa, in turn, is responsible for the areas of police, education, agriculture, industry and public health.

Talaulim

Talaulim is located near Goa Velha by the confluence of the Siridao and Zuari Rivers.

Worth seeing is the **St. Anna Church:** Built in 1695 on the northern bank of the Siridao River, this church is considered an architectural jewel of the Indo-Portuguese baroque by art historians. The church, dedicated to St. Anna, is above all worth seeing because of a structural peculiarity: the walls are hollow so that the worshippers could walk to the confession booths undisturbed.

Talpona

Talpona is a small sailing and fishing harbour in the southern province of Canacona near the mouth of the Talpona River. Due to the extremely shallow water, only flat sailing and fishing vessels can enter this harbour.

Tambdi Surla

Located 23 kilometres west of Ponda in the Sanguem province, the town of Tambdi Surla could only be reached on foot from Sancordem up until recently. The name of this town comes from the colour of its laterite soil — "tambdi" means red.

Tambdi Surla / **Sights**

The only remaining temples of the Kadamba kings are situated in a valley protected by the Westghats. Built in the 12th and 13th centuries, these temples are by far the oldest preserved religious sites in Goa. Their architecture also indicates their age: these temples dedicated to Shiva were built from soft basalt stone.

Meanwhile, the Government has declared the temples of Tambdi Surla a protected national monument. From this point in time, financial subsidies have flowed into the Archaeological Survey of India to make the extensive restoration work possible.

Telephone

Telephone calls to Europe or overseas must be placed by the reception or directly by contacting the operator. Waiting for a connection can take between one and three hours. It usually takes less time during the evening hours. A three-minute call to Europe currently costs around 102 Rs. plus the hotel's surcharge, which varies from hotel to hotel: this can increase the charge to up to 300 Rs. Direct connections are available only at the "O Coqueiro" restaurant, located

in the northern part of Goa on the thoroughfare from Panjim to Mapusa. Demand is accordingly high.
Telegrams can be sent from the hotel reception. These forms (in English) must be filled out legibly in block letters.

Temples

Meanwhile there is once more a Hindu temple in every village, in which the gods are worshipped or prayers for assistance spoken. Shiva, his elephant-headed son Ganesha, Vishnu and the ape god Hanuman play the most important roles in the Indian faith *(→Religion).* An atmosphere of religious tolerance was, however, not always present. When the Portuguese conquered Goa, they quickly began with coercive proselytization under the pressure of the counter-reform. At that time, Many Hindus fled to the secluded, hilly landscape of the Ponda region since this area was first annexed by the colony 250 years later. Those who are already familiar with the major temple complexes in India will discover a different type of temple altogether: halls with pointed gables, red tile roofs and massive towers.
Since each temple is a presentation of the mystic Hindu paradigm, recurring architectural elements can be found in each temple. These elements have been preserved over the years and only varied. The temples portray the world as a rectangle, surrounded by lofty mountains, the temple walls. Adjacent to the complex, outside the temple walls is the ocean of the endless universe, from which all life emanated — symbolized by the temple pond, or "tank," a natural or artificial reservoir. Originally, the temple pond was used only for ritual cleansing and sacrificial ceremonies, but its practicality was quickly recognised by the Hindus, who now use it to wash clothing, dishes and children as well. The actual temple is entered through a main central gateway. Located nearby are usually the drum chambers (nagarkhana), where common temple servants remind that it is once again time for a worship ceremony ("puja"). The pilgrim's quarters, "agrashalas," extend along the temple walls on three sides of the complex. The stone lamp post in the form of steps next to the main hall is called "dipmal" in Goa. The actual temple is distributed among several rooms, the sanctity attributed to each room increasing as one moves on toward the centre. The congregation hall ("sabhamandapa") is often in the form of a gallery of columns. Adjacent to it is the corridor or prayer room ("mandapa") leading to the sanctuary ("antarala"). The most holy of places within the temple, the "cella" with its sanctified cell may only be entered by the priests. In the

''gharbhagriha,'' in English ''uterus,'' there are pictures or statues of the temple's god as well as his symbols. Outside the temple, the location of the most sacred site can be easily recognised: ''shikhara,'' a small tower, that symbolizes the mystical global mountain Meru, rises above the sanctified cell. On the tip of the tower is a water-filled, usually golden sphere, the ''amalaka.'' The Hindus believe this to be a conductor for the divine spark.
Daily at noon, one can witness the ''puja,'' the worship ceremony, which takes place five times a day: at sunrise, during the morning hours, at noon, in the afternoon and at sunset. If an offering is given to the Brahmans (recognised by the white string they wear) in the form of a few Rupees, then non-Hindus can also take part in the ceremony. One takes a sip of the blessed water out of the priest's hand, then, runs one's right hand (the left is considered dirty) lightly from one's forehead over the hair to the back of the neck. The silver statue of the god and the holy flame can then be gazed upon for a few seconds. The whole spectacle is accompanied by loud drum beats and bells. The temple assistants, all from the upper caste of the Brahmans, softly chant traditional ''mantras'' and recite from the sacred scriptures in Sanskrit. In conclusion, the priest dips his finger into a fine powder and places a dark red point on the foreheads of the faithful. This is the ''Tikka,'' the sign of a successful pilgrimage.
→*Holidays and Celebrations*

Theft →*Crime*

Time of Day

The time in Goa is 5.5 hours earlier than in the UK and 10.5 to 13.5 hours earlier than in the continental US. Travelling to Goa, watches must be set ahead; returning, watches must be set back.
During the summer months, the time difference is one hour less.

Tipping →*Bakshish*

Indian women washing in the holy pond in front of the Mangueshi Temple ▶

Tirakol

Tirakol is a small town in the northern extremity of Goa, 42 kilometres from Panjim.

Tirakol / **Sights**

Tirakol Fort: The northernmost Portuguese fortress is perched on a mound composed of red laterite. Built by Bhounsel, this fortress was annexed into the crown colonies by the viceroy Marquis de Alorna in 1746. During the rule of Governor General Bernardo Peres da Silva, Portuguese rebels stormed the fort and massacred all of the soldiers stationed there.
St. Anthony Chapel: The Chapel of Tirakol, founded in 1746 in honour of the holy trinity of father, son and holy ghost, was later dedicated to the national patron saint of Portugal, St. Anthony.
Tirakol Memorial: On September 16, 1954, the National Congress of Goa proclaimed ''satyagraha,“ a non-violent Protest, according to Gandhi's example, to bring about the liberation of Goa. Indians from the neighbouring also took part in this mass demonstration. 15 years later, on September 16, 1969, the ''Goa Freedom Fighter Association“ laid the cornerstone for this memorial in honour of the martyrs of Hirve Guruji and Wadekar, who were killed during this protest.

Tirakol / **Practical Information**

Accommodation: The former fort was made into a simply furnished hotel called the Tourist Rest House; reservations should be sent to: P.O. Kerim Pernem, Goa Reservation Authority Caretaker; single and double rooms as well as a dormitory are available.

Tourist Information

The National Department of Tourism, Government of Goa, Daman & Diu, maintains Tourist Information Offices in:
Panjim: Rue Alfonso de Albuquerque, Tel: 26 73; Interstate Bus Terminus, Counter 5, Tel: 56 20 (9:30 am to 4 pm)
Margao: Municipal Building, Tel: 25 13
Vasco de Gama: Joshi Building, Tel: 26 73
Dabolim Airport: Tourist Information Counter, Tel: 26 44.

Tourist information offices for the neighbouring provinces can also be found in Goa.
For Maharashtra, in Panjim, Tourist Hotel, Tel: 35 72; Interstate Terminus.
For Karnataka, in Panjim, Velho Filhos Building, Tel: 41 10.

Transportation within Goa

Transportation / **By Air**

Dabolim Airport, three kilometres from the harbour city of Vasco and 30 kilometres from the capital of Panjim, was first opened to civil air traffic in 1985. From here, there are daily flights with Indian Airlines from Goa to Bombay, Cochin and Trivandrum. The Indian national airline flies four times a week to and from Bangalore. There are also non-stop flights to Hyderabad and Poona four times a week from Vayudoot.
Tuesdays, Air India flies from Goa via Bombay to Kuwait and Dubai. *Important:* Domestic flights are often fully booked. Tickets should therefore be reserved in advance. Even if the ticket has an "OK" on it, the flight must be reconfirmed before departure; with connecting flights, immediately upon arrival. Delays are typical as are the lengthy security checks, which often take on grotesque dimensions. Most airlines have offices in the larger cities, with inexpensive shuttle service to the airport — far less expensive than taxis. One should have around 300 Rupees ready at departure for the airport tax in Dabolim. The exact fees vary according to the airline and the time of departure (and the mood of the Indian airport personnel).

Airline Offices

Air India: Hotel Fidalgo, 18 June Road, Panjim, Tel: 40 81 (national airline for international air travel).
Indian Airlines: Dempo House, Dayanand Bandodkar Marg, Panjim, Tel: 38 26; 38 31; 40 67. Ticket Counter at Dabolim Airport: Tel: 27 88 (national airline for domestic air travel).
Air France/Bangladesh Biman/British Caledonia Airways/Gulf Air/Philippine Airways: Jesuit House (near the city park), Panjim, Tel: 39 81.
British Airways/Kenya Airways: Chowgule Brothers, across from the Captain of the Ports Office, Panjim Tel: 52 66.
Indonesian Airways/K.L.M.: Thakker Travel Service, Thakker's House, Vasco da Gama, Tel: 28 61.
Kuwait Airways: National Travel Service, Hotel Fidalgo, Room 121, 18th June Road, Tel: 33 21 through 33 29 (eight telephone lines).

Trans World Airlines: Pantours, 8 Junta House, 18th June Road, Panjim, Tel: 47 88.
Vayudoot: United Air Travel, Camila Building (across from the old central bus station), Panjim, Tel: 49 11, 63 36.

Transportation / **By Ship**

The ship passage from Panjim — Bombay with the M/S Mogul Line, which formerly operated regularly, has unfortunately been discontinued.

Transportation / **By Ferry**

Because bridges are still a rarity in Goa, rickety looking boats offer the only reliable ferry service operating regularly. The ferries depart when their capacity is sufficiently occupied — this decision is reached by the captain. **Passenger Ferries** operate on the following routes:

* Dona Paula — Mormugao (only during calm seas): September until May
* Panjim — Aldona: once daily
* Panjim — Britona, Naroa: twice daily
* Panjim — Verem: depending on demand

Ferries with **Vehicle Transportation** operate on the following routes:

* Aldona — Corjuem
* Colvale — Macasana
* Old Goa — Divar
* Panjim — Betim
* Pompurpa — Chorao
* St. Estevam — Tonca
* Siolem — Chopdem
* Keri — Tiracol
* Cortalim — Marcaim
* Narve — Diwar

Transportation / **By Train**

India has almost 60,000 kilometres of railways and over 7,000 train stations, making it the largest railway network in Asia and the fourth largest in the world. Only the USA, USSR and Canada have more extensive rail networks. The train system is the result of the ''Indian Railway“ founded by the British, which expedited the development of the railways during the colonial times.
The train is India's most important means of transportation. Over ten million passengers per day tavel by train. The trains often appear quite archaic: loud,

black, puffing steam locomotives, open doorways (there are no doors) and bars on the windows. There are four travel classes: Air conditioned (A/C), first, second and third class. In A/C and first class, the upholstered seats can be made into a bed in the evening, in the other classes, the seats are simple wooden benches. For all classes, advance reservations are definitely necessary. The names of passengers travelling A/C and first class appear publicly on a list displayed at the train station. One can check the compartment number on this list. The trains travel at a moderate speed, but the landscape can hardly be enjoyed through the barred windows. The prices are astonishingly low by most standards: only £27 ($46) for 1,000 kilometres.

Goa is serviced by the Miraj — Bangalore route of the Southern Central Railways. Larger train stations are found in Vasco, Margao and Mormugao, the last station on this route. There are smaller stations in Cansaulim, Caranzol, Chandor, Colem, Dabolim, Dudhsagar, Majorda, Cuchorem, Seraulim and Sonauli. Panjim is not included in the railway network. Bombay can be reached via Miraj (transfer); the trip lasts around 21 hours. A luxury bus operated by the Kadamba Transport Corporation runs from Margao and Vasco to Bangalore via Karwar. From Bangalore, there are good rail connections to Cochin and the renowned Kerala Beach. To Hospet, the starting point for a tour of the Vijayanagar complex, first take the bus to Hubli, then transfer to the train continuing to Hospet. Information is available and reservations can be made at the train stations (Vasco, Tel: 23 98; Margao, Tel: 2 22 52), in Panjim, at the Interstate Bus Stand and the Out Agency booking Office (Tel: 56 20), located, when coming from the centre of the city, to the right near the Tourist Office (closed Wednesdays and Sundays).

Transportation / **By Bus**

There are two bus terminals in the centre of Panjim, which offer service to destinations within Goa and other states. All local buses travelling north depart from Betim, located on the other side of the Mandovi River (ferry). Shuttle buses run from Mapusa to Anjuna and Vagator Beach. Margao is the best point of departure to travel to the beaches of Goa. The fares are extremely inexpensive. The bus drivers sometimes drive quite unrestrainedly, but are definitely aware of the dimensions of their buses. There are also buses to Bangalore and Bombay among other destinations (travel time: approximately 17 hours). As with trains, advance reservations are definitely necessary. Private long-distance buses are less expensive and more comfortable than the state-run lines. Tickets are available in countless travel agencies.

Locations of the booking agencies for the state-run buses:
Kadamba Transport Corporation, Traffic Office, Bus Stand, Panjim, open daily from 9 am to 6 pm; Karnataka Transport Corporation/Maharashtra Transport Corporation: both offices are located across from the former docks. Open from 8 to 11 am and 2 to 4 pm.

Transportation / **By Taxi**

Taxis are inexpensive in Goa and can therefore also be recommended for longer trips. They, however, can not drive beyond the borders of Goa — special permission is necessary for this. The yellow and black vehicles are the standard taxis in India, old Fiat models built under licence by the Indian automobile manufacturer Pal. The light beige Ambassador models are more expensive, but also offer more comfort. Vehicles and airport taxis belonging to the hotel are the most expensive of the alternatives. As a general rule: trips to the destination and back again are much less expensive than single trips, even when they include longer delays or waiting times. The minimum price for the standard taxis is 3.50 Rupees. Waiting time is charged at 10 Rupees per hour, night rates are charged from 8 pm. Although obligatory, the taximeters are often broken or missing completely. Every driver does however have a list of standard prices, which must be presented upon request.
One should definitely agree upon a price in advance, even when the meter is used. This is also true for the auto-rickshaws and the scooters (small yellow and black, three-wheeled vehicles, whose continual jolting can become quite a "pain in the back" when travelling longer distances). The base price for these types of taxis is 2.50 Rupees. There are often standard prices for the most common destinations.
Now and again, one will also come across the yellow and black motorcycle taxis. According to Indian traffic regulations, only the driver is required to wear a helmet. In practice, however, it is usually casually slung over the handlebars. The driver only puts it on shortly before entering a town.

Transportation / **By Rental Car**

In renting a car, one also hires a driver. There are no rental cars available without a driver. Cars are usually rented out for at least eight hours or 100 kilometres. The following models are available through GTDC, Tourist Home, Panjim, Tel: 33 96, 39 03:
* A/C Deluxe Car: air conditioned luxury car, seats four, 8 Rs./km, 15 Rs. waiting fee/hour, 50 Rs. night surcharge

* A/C Contessa: air conditioned mid-sized car, seats four, 4.50 Rs./km, 15 Rs. waiting fee/hour, 50 Rs. night surcharge.
* A/C Ambassador: roomy mid-sized car with air conditioning, seats four, 4 Rs./km, 15 Rs. waiting fee/hour, 50 Rs. night surcharge
* Ambassador: mid-sized car seating five without air conditioning, 2.50 Rs./km, 10 Rs. waiting fee/hour, 50 Rs. night surcharge.

Groups can rent busses with 15 to 41 seats. The prices per kilometre range between 4.50 and 8.50 Rs. per kilometre; night surcharge, 75 Rs. An additional fee of Rs. 100 is charged if the bus is driven outside of Goa.

Transportation / **By Bicycle**

Bicycles can be rented in all cities, on all of the beaches and in most of the hotels for 6 to 10 Rupees per day. One can also rent a moped or motorcycle for around 100 Rupees and by presenting an international driving licence.

Travel Documents

Tourists must have a valid visa. As a rule, visas are granted for three months. Border officials will send tourists without a visa back on the next plane without batting an eye. Request application forms in writing, including a self-addressed stamped envelope from the Indian Embassy or Consulate in your home country.

In the United States: Embassy of the Republic of India, 2107 Massachusetts Ave. NW, Washington, D.C. 20008-2811, Tel: (202) 939-7000, Fax: (202) 939-7027.

General Consulates:

* in Chicago: 150 N. Michigan Ave., Suite 1100, Chicago, IL 60601-7524, Tel: (312) 781-6280, Fax: (312) 781-6269
* in New York: 3 East 64th Street, New York, NY 10021-7097, Tel: (212) 879-7800, Fax: (212) 988-6423
* in San Francisco: 540 Arguello Blvd., San Francisco, CA 94118-3203, Tel: (415) 688-0662, Fax: (415) 688-2073.

In the United Kingdom: India House, Aldwych, London WC 2B 4NA, Tel: (071) 8368484.

in Australia: 3-5 Moonah Place, Yarralumla ACT 2600, Tel: (062) 733999.

in Canada: 10, Springfield Road, Ottawa K1M 1C9, Tel: (613) 744-3751.

Application Documents:

* two passport photos
* passport, valid for at least six months (children's identification including a passport photo is necessary for children under ten)

* a voucher from a travel agency confirming that a return ticket has been paid, or confirmation from a bank or employer confirming that the living expenses in India can be financed.
* Self-addressed stamped envelope

Processing time: approximately two weeks

Visa fees must be paid upon application by enclosing a check, cashier's check, money order or cash.

→*Customs Regulations, Embassies*

Travel Literature

Manshar Mulgastion/Mario Miranda, *Inside Goa, Latest Tourist Guide Goa,* Asha Publishing House, 1988 (includes good street maps with a scale of 1:200,000 as well as city maps of Panjim and Margao).

TPT Guide Book to Goa, 1987 (succinct guide with a good street map with a scale of 1:160,000, including a general map of Panjim).

Antonio Menezes, *Goa — A Brief Historical Sketch,* AMA Travel Publications, 1988.

Mariano Dias, *Old Goa — Rome of the East,* St. Francis Xavier Centre for the Handicapped, 1987.

Travelling to Goa

There are direct flights from a number of European airports to Dabolim Airport, the gateway to Goa. It is, however less expensive to book a non-stop flight from Europe to Bombay. These flights land at the Sahar International Airport. One can then get a connecting flight from the Santa Cruz Airport to Dabolim. The flight lasts about eight and a half hours from the European continent. The connecting flights to Dabolim last about an hour. Upon departure from India, one must pay an airport tax of 300 Rs. (£ 10, $17). The least expensive way for the individual traveller to get to Goa is usually by purchasing tickets that are available through travel agencies offering student travel. Flights within India are relatively inexpensive. Direct flights from Europe to Bombay cost around £ 480 ($825).

Goa has been a package tour destination since 1987.

Vaccinations →*Medical Care*

Vagator

Located on the mouth of the Chapora River, this former hippie beach can only be reached via an old tar road. This beach has an extremely familiar atmosphere and ''intruders" are eyed critically at first. Although relatively small, the beach is very picturesque.

→*Chapora*

Accommodation: Diamont International: 30 bungalows with shower/toilet, restaurant, bar, tennis courts, approximately 1 km from the beach.

Valpoi

55 kilometres north of Panjim, the small town of Valpoi is a good starting point for a trip to Carambolim, located 7 kilometres away. One of the few remaining Brahma temples in India can be found there.

→*Carambolim*

Accommodation: Valpoi Forest Rest Houses.

Vasco da Gama

Vasco da Gama, situated on the left bank of the Zuari River, is the transportation centre of Goa: the railway ends here, airplanes land at Dabolim and the vessels transporting minerals depart from the harbour in Mormugao.

Vasco / **Practical Information**

Accommodation: *I. Western Style*

Lapaz Hotel, Sawantantry Path, Tel: 21 21 (six telephone lines), Telex: Vision 0191-291, air conditioned.

Hotel Zuari, Tel: 1 27.

Tourist Hotel, Tel: 31 19.

Hotel Annapurna, Tel: 31 85.

Hospital: Tel: 24 54

Pharmacies: Cosme Matias Menezes, near the taxi stand, Tel: 23 64; Menezes & Cia., near the taxi stand, Tel: 26 45; Farmacia Salcete, near Baroda Bank, Tel: 25 81; Farmacia National, near the taxi stand, Tel: 25 88; Farmacia Vasant, near the taxi stand, Tel: 25 11.

Police: Tel: 23 04

Post Office and Telephones: Tel: 27 64

Restaurants: Little Chef Restaurant (fast-food), next to the Cine Vasco.
Restaurant in Hotel Annapurna.
''Nanking,'' Chinese cuisine, next to Hotel La Paz.
Hotel Zuari, excellent but rather expensive.
Tourist Information: Tourist Information Centre, Joshi Building, Tel: 26 73.
Train Station: Tel: 23 98
Transportation: buses depart regularly for Panjim. The trip takes about an hour.
Travel Agencies: West Coast Tours, Vila Rebelo, Mundvel, Tel: 21 10; Merces Travels, 6 Vasco Towers, Tel: 20 77; Rau Raje Desprabhu, Tel: 23 04.

Vasco / **Surroundings**

Mormugao Harbour: →*Mormugao*
Baina Beach: Especially frequented by the natives, Baina Beach is located on the left bank of the Zuari River. Because of the high level of industrialization, it is strongly advised against swimming in the area surrounding Vasco.

Vegetation

Only little is left of the original vegetation in the heavily populated state of Goa. The remnants of what was once the largest monsoon forest on the slopes of the Westghats are now protected by conservation laws. In 1988, the Indian environmentalists marched 1,250 miles to protest against the further deforestation of the Westghats. The unchecked exploitation of the forests, which began during the colonial period, has already transformed the mountain landscape into a desert in some places. Although the extent of the damage in Goa remains relatively limited, the environmental movement began here: Kumar Kalaland Mani organised the 100-day ''Save the Westghats'' march in which 160 environmental groups with over 2000 participants marched. The teak forests, which were cut down by the Portuguese and used in the construction of their caravels, and later used to build the railways, were the focus of this protest. Broad expanses fell victim to the mining of iron ore, bauxite silicates, magnesium and manganese. The intensive cultivation of cotton gradually took over areas where the giant trees once stood with their huge leaves and upright, grape-like fruit stems. Finally, the number of trees is also diminished by nature itself: the trunks and leaves are often infested by termites. Hundreds of the reddish-brown trunks are stacked along the roadways.
In the damper regions of the Westghats, one still finds the impressive bamboo thickets in the undergrowth. These massive wooden ''tubes'' shoot up

to the height of a five-story building. The harvested poles are used in building framework and huts. Baskets are made from the tufts of grass that grow on the upper end of the stalks. However, these primeval bamboo thickets were, over the years, also destined to give way to colonial annexation and agriculture: rice, mangoes, papayas and cashews are still the main agricultural products today. The well-irrigated rice fields, the 100-day rice crops are harvested up to three times a year. Thanks to these crops, the basic sustenance could be ensured for the population. The rice fields are often bordered by palm groves, frequently interspersed with banana and pineapple trees.

The betel palms (Areca catechu) are characterised by their extremely thin, delicate trunks. In November and December, boys climb up the smooth trunks using rope slings to pick the orange betel nuts, swinging from tree to tree. Once harvested, the nuts are then dried and removed from the tough, fibery shell and coarsely chopped. All along the streets, there are peddlers selling mounds of light green tobacco or betel palm leaves. Rolled in these leaves are some gambier resin, salt or sugar and several pieces of betel nut. The ''chewing gum" is then bound by a thin thread. It has the effect of a stimulant, is an appetite suppressant and a disinfectant — after being chewed, the wad is spit with a high arc onto the street. An unmistakable indication of betel nut indulgence is dark red discolouration of the teeth and gums. If used over a longer period, the acids can eat away at the gums, the gums recede and the teeth finally fall out.

In Goa's interior, where the landscape is characterised by laterite rock and bare ground, the Goans are recultivating the eroded slopes with easily tended cashew plantations. The somewhat compact trees are easily recognised by their oval, greenish-yellow leaves and their white blossom stems, on which the bright red, juicy cashew apples grow in February. Within the cashew apple is the actual fruit with its seeds, the cashew ''nut," one of Goa's main export goods. Because the cashew apple contains a pungent juice, the seeds must first be dried or roasted before they can be eaten. It is worth taking a few bags of these nuts home with you. In Goa they cost only about one-tenth of the normal price and can be purchased in a number of forms: raw, roasted, salted or seasoned with masala spices (hot)...

Mangoes are at least as widely spread. This agricultural plant originates from Eastern India. Over 500 species of mangoes can be found in Goa. All of these ripen shortly before the rainy season at the end of March or beginning of April. Papayas, also called melon trees, can often be found in the front gardens of the old colonial villas. The green peel containing orange fruit is harvested during the entire year. In addition, the largest fruit in the world, the yak-fruit, is also

endemic to Goa. The squash-like type of breadfruit can grow to be as heavy as twelve pounds. Deliciously prepared as a vegetable, it often goes unrecognised as the "Indian potato."
A wide-spread botanical peculiarity in Goa is the bayan tree with its broad, sweeping branches, from which aerial roots hang. If the roots reach the ground, then a new tree sprouts. A number of these off-shoots can cause a confused tangle of trunks and branches — the older the grove, the more impenetrable. The trees are, however, usually pruned regularly by the natives, who use the roots as fire wood.

Vela Goa →*Old Goa*
Visas →*Travel Documents*
Weather →*Climate*

Wildlife and Animals

Ravens and cranes are, with the exception of insects, the most common animals: they take on the role of the thieving magpie in Goa. Open hotel windows are an irresistible temptation for them. In the wink of an eye, they snatch jewellry and other shiny objects. Thus, many a hotel theft is exposed as an ornithological affair.
The apes are by no means any less adroit than the feathered thieves. They are particularly partial to snatching the shoes, which were removed by the temple visitors. There is only one thing that can be done about this: use a stick or rock to stage a mock attack. When the apes flee, they usually drop everything in fright. By no means should one try to grab the stolen goods from the apes — they defend "their" possessions by biting, which can be very painful. Langurs, Gibbons and long-tailed monkeys can be observed most often; they enjoy sitting in the trees along the roads. With a few nuts or roasted beans, one can quickly tempt them out of their perch.
The white Indian zebu cow with its prominent hump, ideally suited for harnessing, can also bee seen throughout Goa. They can even be found in the cities, where they wander about the marketplaces in search of food. They will stick their open mouths into the kitchens, before being driven away by the peddlers with a flurry of curses. If a cow lies down in the middle of the road, then nothing can be done except waiting or formulating a few convincing arguments for the cow. Whoever runs into a cow, must count on a very high fine; if the cow

is killed, then severe prison sentences result. The cow has been sacred in India for more than three thousand years. This started with the immigration of the Aryans into the Indus valley: this was the only way to ensure that their own sustenance was not destroyed. The milk from the cow was an important contribution to their nourishment, the urine disinfected with its high concentrations of ammonia, and the cow chips — available at the markets for a few Rupees — were used as a fuel for fires. In its "raw" form, cow dung is excellent for plastering houses. In Pompurpa, one inventive "hotel" owner even made a bench from cow dung. Used in ploughing the fields or transporting grain, the zebu accomplishes the most diverse tasks. In addition, feeding the cow is quite uncomplicated — one merely sends it away to find its own food. Also commonly found in Goa is the black water buffalo, which can be seen tirelessly pulling the archaic wooden ploughs through the water-laden rice fields, stopping at even the smallest of puddles to cool themselves. Since water buffaloes have no sweat glands, they would otherwise die of heat prostration. Living in the two national parks in the Westghats, there are still over 80 wild gaurs, an Indian race of buffalo. There are also a number of poisonous snakes in Goa, but the widespread fear of them is not founded: they are very sensitive to sound. But do be careful with termites. Their nests are a favourite hiding place for cobras, as are the rice fields. An old legend recounts:

The princess Shri Devi fell in love one day with the handsome king of the rice fields; this, against her father's will. Angered, he turned his daughter into a cobra. When the spell had taken effect, she found herself on the ground in the middle of a rice field. The farmer, who owned the field, was of course happy to have the guest, which killed all of the unwelcome rodents, thus ensuring him a record harvest. Gradually, the villagers became sceptical. They resolved to uncover the farmer's secret. They observed in astonishment how the farmer spoke to the snake, brought it small offerings and adorned it with flowers. The next day, all of the rice fields in the village — and shortly thereafter, all of the rice fields in India — had a small temple decorated with flowers and containing offerings for Shri Devi. Curious, as snakes tend to be, Shri Devi left the rice field. From that day on, no one knows exactly where Shri Devi is...

In many areas, one will also see radiant white birds in the bright green rice fields looking for food: these are cattle egrets, which spend the winter here. Sprightly green parrots can often be seen near the temple complexes; here and there, one might see the majestic kingfisher, with its dark blue feathers, perched on a telegraph pole. The vultures take on the role of the pestilence patrol: they eat the cadavers of animals killed on the roads in a matter of minutes.

Crocodiles, elephants, tigers and panthers, animals which simply belong to the conceptual picture of India, can only be found in Goa's zoos. In Bondla Wildlife Park, the plague of the western city sits cooing behind thick bars — the European pigeon. However, common all over Goa is an animal to which Remo, Goa's internationally successful pop star, dedicated a parody: ''The Goan Pig.'' The young animals can easily be mistaken for a dog as they run through the streets of the villages; full grown, they have a similarity with a domesticated wild boar. The pink farmyard pig was first imported to Goa in the 18th century.

Zambaulim

Zambaulim is 22 kilometres south of Margao in the Sanguem province.
Worth seeing is the **Shri Damodar Temple:** Built in an idyllic location on the banks of the Kushvati River, this temple is also called Panti by the natives. The river is considered sacred by the Hindus and Christians alike because the water is said to have healing properties. The week-long Holi festival, called ''Shigmo'' in Goa, is held here.